Chasing Rainbows

Finding Beauty in Life's Storms

Rachelle Van Ryssen

www.SIMPinc.info
SIMPI
Sisters Ignited Media Publishing Inc
Book Publisher
226-931-4059

Sisters Ignited Media and Publishing Inc.

Cover Design by Khristien Van Ryssen.

All bible quotes are from the New International Version or New King James Version unless otherwise indicated.

Dedication:

To my friends and contributing authors

"CHASING RAINBOWS"

Finding Beauty in Life's Storms

I WOULD LIKE TO dedicate this book to all the women who have blessed us with their very personal stories. Thank you for agreeing to be part of the inaugural "Chasing Rainbows" book, in what I believe the Lord will bless to be the first in many more *Rainbow Chasing* stories!

Thank you to our families for your support and encouragement. Thank you for all of the prayers! Thank you, God, for turning our storms into rainbows.

A special thank you to Wendy Noll for all her work and Khristien Van Ryssen for the cover design.

Thank you to our contributing authors in order of their Chapters:

Karen deBlieck - "Fractured Rainbows"
Ann Reid - "The Eye of the Storm"
Cheryl Weber - "Joy Comes in the Morning"
Lisa Nigh - "In His Word I Hope"
Rachelle Van Ryssen - "Some Rainbows Take Time"
Beverly Hadland - "Rainbows during COVID"
Michelle Sim - "My Storm Has a Name"
Beth Fisher - "The Final Answer to Every Question"
Penny MacCormack - "Strength, Determination, Focus and Faith"
Sarah VanNetten - "COVID, Chicken and a Miracle"
Jill Cornell - "The Road Home"
Tamara Hiller - "Divorce, Lilacs, Whispers and my Friend Elijah"

Introducion

By Rachelle Van Ryssen / CEO of Sisters Ignited Media and Publishing Inc.

GREETINGS! MY NAME IS Rachelle Van Ryssen, and I would like to introduce you to the first of a series of anthologies called, "Chasing Rainbows."

I am inspired to say that we are blessed to be able to bring you this amazing book. It is filled with the most inspirational stories by fourteen women who have been thrust into some of the worst storms in life. They were each chosen and invited to share their personal stories of hope and finding the beauty in the tempests.

If you are prepared to see past the darkness in your life and join us as a "Rainbow Chaser," then this book is for you!

The inception of this book was without a doubt inspired from above. I truly believe that it was a Devine commission given by a loving Father.

A few years ago, while navigating a difficult diagnosis and subsequent surgery, my husband / best friend and I went for a drive during a summer storm. The rain was pounding down on the vehicle and the sky was black and grey. We could see slight wisps of light trying to crack through the darkness.

'John and I take nightly drives to unwind and get caught up on our day.'

As we were driving through our beautiful community the storm suddenly lifted the sky broke open and a rainbow appeared, then another and yet another!

We drove out of Simcoe, my hometown and toward our favourite spot to relax with a tea at the pier in Port Dover, Ontario.

As we entered the town, we spotted several more rainbows! They were everywhere! Multiple, beautiful promises from God for better days come.

As we drove, I nonchalantly said, *"we are Rainbow Chasers! Some people chase storms, we have always chased the rainbows."*

Then I looked over at John and said, *"Man, that would be a great idea for a book, "Chasing Rainbows!"*

And so, the idea was born.

I later prayed about it and realized that this book would be written by several diverse women. These women would bare their souls through their stories of surviving, ordeals, loneliness, sickness, loss and seemingly impossible circumstances.

The women in this anthology are from all walks of life. Their experiences are raw and authentic. They are all just trying to walk with God and live their lives well. Each of them is inspiring and the kind of women we all need to have in our lives. The type of women who get joy from seeing other people find their rainbows.

So let this book be a comfort and a friend to you as you read our stories.

Each of us has reached deeply into some difficult times and dark areas of their life to share our breakthroughs and discoveries with you.

We all must face storms! But we don't have to do it alone.

'So, grab a warm drink, get comfortable and cuddle up somewhere cozy. Get ready to make a few new friends. It's time to chase some rainbows!'

I would like to introduce you to the first of a series of anthologies called, "Chasing Rainbows."

I am inspired to say that we are blessed to be able to bring you this amazing book. It is filled with the most inspirational stories by fourteen women who have been thrust into some of the worst storms in life. They were each chosen and invited to share their personal stories of hope and finding the beauty in the tempests.

If you are prepared to see past the darkness in your life and join us as a "Rainbow Chaser," then this book is for you!

The inception of this book was without a doubt inspired from above. I truly believe that it was a Divine commission given by a loving Father.

A few years ago, while navigating a difficult diagnosis and subsequent surgery, my husband / best friend and I went for a drive during a summer storm. The rain was pounding down on the vehicle and the sky was black and grey. We could see slight wisps of light trying to crack through the darkness.

'John and I take nightly drives to unwind and get caught up on our day.'

As we were driving through our beautiful community the storm suddenly lifted the sky broke open and a rainbow appeared, then another and yet another!

We drove out of Simcoe, my hometown and toward our favourite spot to relax with a tea at the pier in Port Dover, Ontario.

As we entered the town, we spotted several more rainbows! They were everywhere! Multiple, beautiful promises from God for better days come.

As we drove, I nonchalantly said, *"we are Rainbow Chasers! Some people chase storms, we have always chased the rainbows."*

Then I looked over at John and said, *"Man, that would be a great idea for a book, "Chasing Rainbows!"*

And so, the idea was born.

I later prayed about it and realized that this book would be written by several diverse women. These women would bare their souls through their stories of surviving, ordeals, loneliness, sickness, loss and seemingly impossible circumstances.

The women in this anthology are from all walks of life. Their experiences are raw and authentic. They are all just trying to walk with God and live their lives well. Each of them is inspiring and the kind of women we all need to have in our lives. The type of women who get joy from seeing other people find their rainbows.

So let this book be a comfort and a friend to you as you read our stories.

Each of us has reached deeply into some difficult times and dark areas of their life to share our breakthroughs and discoveries with you.

We all must face storms! But we don't have to do it alone.

'So, grab a warm drink, get comfortable and cuddle up somewhere cozy. Get ready to make a few new friends. It's time to chase some rainbows!'

Contents

Chapter One

Fractured Rainbows

Karen deBleick

FOR MOST OF MY life, I felt broken. Incomplete. Like a jigsaw puzzle with missing pieces or a kite without a string, as if the slightest breeze would raise me up and scatter my broken fragments abroad. Untethered. Perhaps it was due to my closed adoption. Perhaps because my dark skin and broad face would never resemble the rest of my family. Whatever the cause, the results were the same. Imperceptible cracks snaked under my skin.

As a preschooler, my days were filled with laughter and dreams. Everyone cooed at my chubby legs and bulldog cheeks. But when I attended elementary school, I learned the sharp truth. Those who I deemed friends viewed me as lesser, and soon I began to question my value.

When you live in a small community, entire classrooms receive invitations to events. Birthday parties and playdates filled the calendar. My last-minute invitations, however, always made me question if I was welcome. Playing line tag meant I had to be "it" five times, no matter how many people I tagged. I was an anomaly—the social rules warped around me. An outcast, the girls treated me differently.

Always the last in line.

Crack.

Always the last one chosen.

Crack.

And I didn't know why.

I tried to be likeable. After all, it must be my fault. I must be doing something wrong. To protect myself, I escaped into books. I created a world where I was wanted and loved.

By grade six the cracks deepened. Classmates paired up and switched partners weekly as they engaged in the dance of "going out." No one ever went anywhere—my classmates had designed a juvenile hierarchy. I remained the odd one out. No one found me attractive. My dark skin marked me as undesirable.

Crack.

My sense of self warped. My parents', progressive as they were, didn't "see colour." My brother and I, both unrelated, were bookended by my adoptive parent's biological children. I believe my parents adopted me with loving intention, but they didn't know what they were getting themselves into. They didn't think racism was morally right, so they chose not to see it. Not out of malice, but rather a belief that if they acknowledged the evil, it meant they accepted it. For me, it made the world harder to understand. It left me with nowhere to turn when I overheard a father and son call me an unknown word. A word filled with venom.

Crack.

Even my home life felt foreign. I knew my parents loved me; they chose me at birth. But they knew nothing of my identity aside from my obvious cuteness. I questioned whether they would have taken me home, had they known all my flaws. Their home, with so many words left unspoken, pressed in on me. I existed in excess—too much, too loud, and too dramatic.

Seeking my birth mother was never something I desired. She must have had a reason for giving me up at birth. Still, I longed for a safe place—a home. At night the train whistle's plaintive call made my heart swell with need. Surely, just beyond the horizon, there was a place for me.

Crack.

Music wove itself into my life, it hid me from the forceful gales and provided comfort. My music teacher, Mrs. MacIntosh, knew of my struggles. So, when I chose to belt out lyrics in music class, she'd comment on how lovely my voice was. My thirsty soul lapped up every word despite the rift it caused amongst my peers. A small gift to hold close.

Every year our school produced a musical. The director cast grade six students in the major roles. The Wizard of Oz, Bambi, and Cinderella—fancy fairy tales filled with beautiful creatures. I dreamt of the day that I could stand centre stage and shine as the main character. Finally, my turn arrived, I auditioned and earned the lead! Joy flooded my heart. Finally! But joy turned to despair when I learned the main character was an old wizard who sang the "Getting Older Blues," with a cloak and a gray beard. Not princessy. Not beautiful. Sure, I spent the most time on the stage, but the snickers and jeers from my classmates cast a shadow on the spotlight. I envied the students who didn't have to hide beneath a fake beard.

Crack.

The winds changed and I braced myself.

Crack.

We graduated from elementary school into junior high and my old "friends" settled into a higher societal tier than me in school. A dark, unsettled cloud grew inside of me. Demons whispered lies. *You're pathetic. Unloved. Dirty. Different.*

Crack.

At this school, I no longer stood out as the only black kid; but the others all had black families at home. They participated in school activities and had friends, yet they lived in another world with their own people. They had a home foundation on which they built their confidence and found their strength and purpose.

My mother, sensing my turmoil, tried everything in her power to help me fit in. On my twelfth birthday she took me to get my hair done at a fancy beauty salon. My very first Jheri curl! She dropped me off at the salon and I spent the day enveloped in the black world. I sat and watched, with my heart full, as black women came and went, visiting and gossiping with each other. A life force pulsed, filling me with joy as I observed my surroundings. And no one questioned whether I belonged.

Until my mother walked in.

Everything shifted. The chatter subsided. When they realized I belonged to *her* they couldn't wait for me to leave. We left so abruptly I never learned how to maintain my hair. Within a week it returned to its unruly frizzy state.

Crack.

I was a misfit in both the black and white worlds. I was adrift. Alone. I didn't belong, so I drew a clear division between me and others. I hung out with a rough crowd and tried to fill the God-sized hole in my heart with love and acceptance. My friend's parents marvelled at my polite mannerism and helpfulness. I would do anything for those I considered friends. And I soaked up any attention from boys.

'After all, how could anyone love me?'

So, when trauma caused our family to move six hours away, even as I shed tears for my childhood home, a part of me was ready for a fresh start.

I arrived in my new hometown three days before I started grade nine. I had to choose a school based on hearsay. According to the neighbours, the school down the road had regular (false) bomb threats. The school across town had a French immersion program and an amazing music department. Limited options minimized my choices.

The first day hit like a slap in the face. I'd chosen a very preppy school. On the first day of class a group of girls called me a slut because I wore a mini skirt. Many of the students had grown up together which made me an outcast. Once again, black students were not held in prestige like hard-working Asian or Indian students. I was beneath them.

At this point, I felt torn by external expectations and judgment. White people disliked the colour of my skin. Black people disliked my white mannerisms and speech. And after a ten-year sabbatical, my father had taken his place as minister in the United Church and expected good behaviour as a 'Preacher's Kid.'

I found a group of misfits and a quirky best friend who loved me. We weren't the most popular or the prettiest, but we shared a mutual loyalty.

I discovered that I wasn't as "naturally talented" at singing as Mrs. Macintosh had me believe. So, I worked hard to become a part of the music department. After several failed auditions, I became a true music geek. My fellow musicians, and teachers became a second family, claiming every spare moment in rehearsals or hanging out in the music room.

My new house was, quite literally, on the wrong side of the tracks and it reminded me of my old home. There, among my second group of friends, I could reveal my rougher side. Despite finding my way at school there was still a longing to know more about my black roots. I was introduced to the underground Trinidad and Jamaican communities. I began staying out late, smoking, drinking and dancing at after hour clubs with men much older than me. Exploring a whole new world, I gave pieces of myself despite the risks and dangers.

On Sunday mornings, I occupied a seat in a church pew and served tea at the women's breakfast. In my eyes, the church functioned as a social club. The congregants didn't read the Bible outside of Sunday service and sermon morals dissipated with the closing of the church doors. And so, like them, I played my part. I knew that God existed, however, His existence had minimal bearing on my day-to-day life.

I juggled my partners in a perpetual dance, aware of the cracks, brokenness, and imperfections. I kept the storms at bay. I was in control. I was safe.

Or so I thought.

I believed myself invincible—living moment to moment. I played with fire, ignoring the danger until I was burned.

Just one night. That's all it took to undo it all.

One night. I whispered no, and a man I considered a friend didn't listen. Although my faith in God was as tentative as a flickering candle, I'd protected it. Now, the flame was snuffed out.

The cracks deepened, and the pain threatened to overtake me. But I held it together—I smiled at school, sang in the choir and sat in my pew on Sundays. No one knew that a piece of me stood in the shower trying to wash away the violation.

I began a relationship with a boy at my high school. He was an awkward but precocious boy. Safe. He gave me exactly what I needed: a cocoon far away from the world. But in addition to wanting a girlfriend, he wanted someone to introduce him to a secretly desired social life. As he grew in confidence, he realized I couldn't survive without him. I needed him more than he needed me. Modelling behaviour from his abusive father, he treated me with disdain. His condescending words sliced my battered soul. His actions confirmed the belief that had taken root in my heart. ***Worthless. Stupid. Lesser.*** When he grew tired, he dumped me, leaving me fragmented in the wake of his rejection.

The descent was slow but assured. A forgotten homework assignment.

Crack.

Staying out past curfew.

Crack.

Showing up for work reeking of yesterday's buzz.

Crack.

Drinking until I should have been legally dead.

Crack.

Recklessly giving myself to men because none of it mattered anymore. Nothing mattered

Crack.

Staying in bed because I was sick. And staying in bed. And staying in bed. And staying in bed—beneath the blankets, blotting out the world.

Crack.

Ashamed, I buried the secret and it festered until I was slickened with its foulness. When I confessed to my best friend, she faltered, not knowing what to say. After sharing with my father, he put on his pastoral façade, and took me to see a doctor and offered to find a counsellor. All I wanted was my dad to hold me in my grief as my insides shattered. Darkness spilled out, colouring my entire world. I hit bottom, and the world dimmed. I wondered if I should continue breathing.

At my lowest, I sensed a nudge when I saw a poster stapled to the church's bulletin board. A local Christian summer camp was looking for counsellors. It was a whim. A moment, perhaps, where I heard God's small voice and listened. The vetting process was thorough, but I knew the correct answers to the questions even if I didn't believe them.

I stepped out of my norms and into something new. I hoped this move might fix me, bind together what had broken, and provide a refuge from the outside world. Give me time to catch my breath. But it wasn't easy.

Is it ever?

The other camp workers welcomed me into their world with an acceptance I had never experienced before. But still, I felt like an onlooker. I saw their daily joy, and I attempted to mimic it, but it wouldn't take root. I remained empty except for a longing to obtain their joy and wisdom.

I believed they would shun me if they knew my story, but transparency was the only way I thought I'd be free. I thought it might lighten the load to share my pain with others. They didn't reject me. In fact, they embraced me, pulling me close. But I didn't find the joy or comfort I expected. Something was missing.

One night, I approached the director and asked how I could have the joy she and others exuded. She said there was only one way. I had to pray to Jesus, confess my sins, and give my life to Him. I closed my eyes as she guided my prayer. The words tasted foreign but sweet on my lips, and my burden lightened.

That summer, my life changed. A profound shift in my worldview evolved. I realized I was adopted into a whole new family. And though the world might let me down countless times, God never would. That summer, I lived in Jesus.

Going back to the real world with its temptations and distractions, was hard. Without the support of a faithful church family or believing friends, I stumbled. But I continually picked myself up. As time passed, the newfound joy seemed to dissipate.

I believed that God would fix me and take all my cracks. That, with Him, I would be made flawless and whole. A smooth pebble, weathered by storms, belonged among the sea of believers.

While that was true, on some level, my experience declared a fuller truth. As time flew by, the pain lessened, and my value as a child of Christ grew. I began to see that my brokenness was a blessing.

Something miraculous happened with every passing year. I travelled through life *with* God. As I grew, each crack and blemish created something beautiful.

Miscarriage.

Crack.

Breast cancer diagnosis. Marriage difficulties. Children with special needs.

Crack. Crack. Crack.

Each painful trial became bearable when I understood that God remained by my side in every storm.

But God had plans for me. I once used books to escape, now I write to process my journey. As I share stories of characters searching amid the darkness, I mirror my journey to find hope and love. My words are for the fractured and broken. Words I wish had been spoken to me. Comfort from my Father.

'*You are loved. You are worthy. You are beautiful. No matter how far you run, I'm here. Come home.*'

My daily prayer is that others learn that, during their most violent storms, the sun is only hidden momentarily. And that family can consist of people with whom you share blood, home or faith.

Now, when God's perfect light shines on my fractured life, beautiful prisms appear. Rainbows declare God's promise. As I share of God's transforming power, I witness projections of prisms and rainbows in others. The world wrote scars on our souls that became a testament to God's faithfulness—even in the darkest hours.

I'd be lying if I said I am always thankful for painful lessons and brokenness. Some days I pick up the ancient burden I left at the cross until the still small voice coaxes it from my arms yet again. Other days, I forget who I am and listen to the lies of my past. Turning to His Word, I arm myself with the promises of His perfect character. I remind myself that despite the cracks, God will reveal Himself in the rainbow—He is faithful and always present.

So, here I stand. Cracked open, yet whole. The crevices filled by God, who loves me wholly and completely. He doesn't see the ugliness of my sin but rather the beauty of who He declares me to be in Christ.

Perfect, beautiful, and His.

Love Karen

Chapter Two

Eye of the Storm

Ann Reid

THE WORLD'S WORST TEMPERED lake, the 11th largest lake in the world, is a lake feared most by Great Lake sailors and is nicknamed "Lake Dreary." It forms the boundary between Canada (Ontario) to the north and the United States (Michigan, Ohio, Pennsylvania, and New York) to the west, south, and east. The shallowest of all the Great Lakes, it has been described as a gigantic puddle, with an average depth of fifty-eight feet.

The tribe of Native Americans and French communities who lived along its southern shore called the lake, "Chat" which translates to the "cat," because of its unpredictable and sometimes violently dangerous nature. Lake Erie's name is derived from *"erielhonan,"* which is Iroquoian for "long tail."

Southwesterly winds produce high waves, white caps, and extremely rough waters. Its raging storms have claimed no less than 1,400 ships and an estimated high of 8,000. Some say this lake has more "wrecks per square mile" than any other freshwater location on earth. The name of this great lake is none other than Lake Erie.

It was a beautiful warm, sunny day on June 28, 2014. My brother, David, and his friend, Irvin, were headed to Simcoe with his boat. He called me on route, advising us to meet him at Turkey Point Marina to help launch the boat into the water.

He planned a fun adventure to celebrate the end of a school year for my husband, Jonathan, and me both elementary school teachers, and our three children—Madison (14), Callum (12), and Evan (9).

During the spring of my final high school year, I camped at the tip of Long Point with my geography class. My brother heard about the school trip and dreamt of visiting the tip of Long Point.

We arrived at the marina, then unloaded the lifejackets and supplies, and carried them down to the dock. David was lowering the boat into the water. It was a modest, 17 ft bow rider. The name "Blue Monday" was etched into the back of the boat. It was the perfect day; clear blue skies, a warm breeze, and the sun glistening atop the gentle ripples that blanketed the lake. As we headed down the channel toward the lake, the music played, and we embraced the fresh air on route to Pottahawk Point.

Pottahawk Point is a small island about 8.5 km southeast of Turkey Point. It is a popular destination for boaters and is only accessible by water.

We stopped at Pottahawk to enjoy snacks and a few drinks. While there, we bumped into a friend who lent us their inflatable raft. David tied it onto the back of his boat and offered the kids a ride.

About an hour later, we ventured out for the 10 km trip to our destination—the tip of Long Point. Closer to the point, there are submerged sand bars which can be treacherous to navigate. David began charting, but the markers didn't line up. He approached the tip slowly and with caution. David was keen to note the water's surface behaviours and changing tints (i.e., clear water) which helped navigate our location.

At one point, the boat gave a sudden jolt and bang. David stopped the boat for inspection. He concluded that the propeller hit the top of a sandbar. The jolt caused the motor to cut out, and it took a few minutes to get it restarted. Eventually, we reached the point.

Long Point is the world's longest freshwater sand spit and extends 40 km on the north shore of Lake Erie. It is a world-class biosphere for migratory birds and wildlife. The very tip houses a historical landmark with a lighthouse and presents a beautiful, secluded paradise.

We anchored the boat and waded through the shallow warm waters to the tip of the point—a 0.3 km trek. We swam, examined bird tracks in the sand, and were mesmerized by the movement of the water cascading from two sides of the point. We noticed the variance in water temperature—the bayside being deeper and more relaxed. We climbed over logs, checked the bird observatory station, and investigated numerous marsh plants.

Approximately half an hour into our exploration of the tip, we heard a faint rumble afar off but attributed it to the loud motor of a passing boater. Hearing a second rumble a few minutes later, we decided to head back to the boat.

The skies were blue, and the sun was shining. A faint breeze was present, and the water was calm. We noticed other boaters packing up and skedaddling. Two other boats were docked beside ours when we arrived at the boat.

We asked one couple, "Did you hear the rumble? Should we stay on the island or head back?"

They said, "We are planning on heading back. There is lots of time."

Other boaters arrived and mentioned they were planning on staying at the point. Based on our observations, we made an executive decision to depart for Turkey Point. We quickly boarded and headed across the waters. Typically, you travel along the shoreline with the threat of an incoming storm. However, with sandbars, this is impossible. We decided to trail the big boat that left before us.

About 10 minutes into our return journey, we heard a loud rumble, and the wind started picking up. The children were wearing lifejackets. Irvin opened the seat hatch at the back of the boat and passed life jackets to Jonathan, David, and me.

Jonathan moved to the boat's bow and straddled the width to add weight and balance to offset the rising waters. He instructed Callum to sit on the floor of the boat. I held Evan and Madison tightly in my lap. Irvin was at the stern of the boat, balancing the other side.

It appeared the air current was quickening. We looked skyward and saw enormous dark black and green-tinged clouds moving quickly and treacherously towards us.

I remember thinking, "Come on, boat, we need to move faster and beat this oncoming storm."

No such luck. Within seconds, a massive gust of wind appeared unexpectedly and ripped the canvas Bimini off the steel rods, lashing it aggressively into the water. Giant balls of hail pelted down, hitting our shivering bodies. The wind's howl grew increasingly loud. Pangs of thunder cracked and boomed uncontrollably. The waves formed foaming ice-cap whirlpools around the stern. The fog crept in, and we lost our bearings. David slowed the speed of the boat to increase safety as he rode the 12-foot waves. The big boat we were following disappeared into the fog.

At one point, David looked back to check on us. I remember locking eyes as I masked a brave face and an encouraging smile. Suddenly, a raging wall of weather gushed starboard, and his hat was tossed 100 feet into the air.

Teeming rain poured into the boat—our ankles already covered in water. David, now hatless, struggled to navigate the route through sheets of torrential rain and wave drifts.

Our clothes, jackets, and towels were drenched. Evan's lips and skin were turning blue. Direct skin-to-skin contact was the only way to attempt to remain warm. All had an eerily silence and stillness.

The waves continued to rage. At times, the water sloshed the side of the boat, and it felt like we were going to capsize. With the onset of each wave, David pulled back on the throttle to steady the boat. With each throttle thrust, my heart leaped into my throat as I catastrophized about the engine cutting out.

I silently panicked. Presenting a calm external facade, my internal state was an emotional mess. My mind raced as I uttered inaudible screams. Observing the churning waters, I realized, despite life jackets, the likelihood of surviving 12-foot waves was slim.

I imagined the devastation my parents would experience if they lost their entire family. They lost my 19-year-old brother in a tragic accident; I couldn't fathom how they'd cope.

Glancing at Jonathan, I contemplated a game plan in the event we were capsized I would hold our kids while holding the boat. The wind and thunder roared, challenging any opportunity to engage in audible communication. We were alone, amidst a tumultuous lake, in the eye of a vicious storm.

We did not have a radio onboard to contact the Coast Guard. Jonathan tightly held on to the bow to brace himself as two monstrous walls of grey water towered on either side of the boat. There are no words that can adequately explain our experience.

Panic heightened to uncontainable levels, my eyes shifted downwards, and I experienced catatonia.

Callum crouched on the floor; hands clasped together praying! During the height of a violent storm, my child demonstrated what he needed to do. I closed my eyes and prayed. Feeling the boat rock in rhythmic synchronicity with the water, I begged God to keep us safe. I asked God to calm the raging storm and guide us to safety.

My eyes remained shut, seemingly forever and a day. I asked God for His peace that transcended understanding and expressed I was unprepared to leave our earthly world. There was much to do, and I longed for time with Jonathan and our children.

I opened my eyes, the storm had not subsided, but it had changed. Numerous lightning bolts struck the water within meters of us. A solitary object in the water, I anticipated us being hit and vaporized. Despite the terror, there was an uncanny beauty amongst multiple flashes of light. To this day, I believe God showered us with a magnificent display of fireworks.

Miraculously, the lightning storm subsided, and the sky became lighter. The wind died down to that of gentle rocking. I felt God's presence—a calming, temperate desire to lull us. Taking a deep breath, I inhaled a glimmer of hope.

The storm clouds and rumbling subsided, the rain dissipated to mist, and sun rays burst through the clouds. In the distance, there appeared a faint hint of land; my brother stared in disbelief. Unbeknownst to us, we maintained a course toward Turkey Point.

As my eyes followed the coastline, I blinked in disbelief. God's promise lay directly in front of us. The most beautiful rainbow I have ever witnessed.

As we headed into the channel, my body shook, and tears streamed down my cheeks. I thanked God for His guidance, grace, power, and unfailing love.

When asked to be a contributing author for "Chasing Rainbows," I initially experienced self-doubt.

I asked myself, "How do the storms in my life compare to others? Surely, others have experienced worse?"

My story was cliché—an actual storm and an actual rainbow. I did not choose to chase either, but I realize they were harrowing, life-changing experiences in hindsight. Weathering this storm changed my life forever.

Post-storm, I experienced PTSD and had to work through bouts of anxiety and recurring nightmares. I believe God knew of this coming storm and embraced our family until it passed. He was, is, and always will be our rock.

I witnessed first-hand the God of miracles. This storm demonstrated the power of prayer and prepared my heart to war in prayer for others as they endure the storms of life.

Some of my favourite verses that I revisit during life's storms are:

1. Psalm 62:1-2 "*My soul finds rest in God alone, my salvation comes from Him, He alone is my rock and salvation.*"

2. Psalm 56:3 "*When I am afraid, I put my trust in you.*"

3. Matthew 19:26 "*With God, all things are possible.*"

4.

Ephesians 3:2 "*God can do exceedingly abundantly above all we think or imagine.*"

5. Isaiah 41:10 "*Don't panic, I am with you. There's no need to fear FOR I'm your God. I'll give you strength. I'll help you. I'll hold you steady, keep a firm grip on you.*"

6. Philippians 4:13 "*Whatever I have, wherever I am, I can make it through anything in the One who makes me who I am.*"

Upon reflection, I realized the inevitable reality that no one is exempt from the storms in life. Although they vary in intensity and duration, we are not left alone to weather them.

I believe God sends storms to encourage growth. They shape us and assist us in identifying our values. God is ever present, despite our inability to see or feel Him. He promises to comfort, protect and love us. Jesus will calm the waves or be with us amongst the storms.

When I recall the experience on Lake Erie, I envision Callum praying. God used a child to demonstrate His power and peace, to lean on Him amid chaos.

I pray that you feel the love of God as you weather the storms in life; and know you aren't alone. There is ONE who works ongoing for your good. Keep looking up—you will find your rainbow.

In His Love, Ann

Chapter Three

Joy Comes in the Morning

Cheryl Weber

IT ALL BEGAN WITH a simple prayer, one that would dramatically change my life. I heard a speaker talk about God in a way that was foreign to me. I didn't agree with his theology, but his approach and relational friendship with God sparked my curiosity. He expressed daily engagement with God and offered many unusual stories to support his allegations. His words were fresh and his perspective unique. It brought to mind, Isaiah 55:8-9, *"For my thoughts are not your thoughts, neither are your ways my ways," declares the Lord. As the heavens are higher than the earth, so are my ways higher than your ways and my thoughts than your thoughts."*

My main argument was centred around his approach to suffering. He encouraged a faith filled response to suffering and accepted it as part of the Christian life. My theological understanding was formed around the idea that walking with God denoted blessing and healing. Suffering encompassed a brief time between the enemy's attack and receiving a blessing. It was hinged on the idea that suffering presented in two ways: when fighting for the answer to prayer or when being persecuted for your faith. I was a bit offended at the speaker's approach yet drawn to an intuitive sense that his words were fresh from heaven.

Although strange, it's difficult to articulate how I knew he was different.

As the result of this experience, I prayed a dangerous prayer. I'm not sure I would do it again, although the fruit of it has been foundational for my life and work with those who are oppressed.

Here's what I prayed, "God, I want to know You, not through my specific theological bent or within the realm of my comfort levels. I want to know You genuinely and authentically."

There was a hunger for truth deep within, beyond tradition, training, or comfort. This man's intimacy with God opened my eyes to MORE!

A few months had passed before the answer to my prayer presented. It all began with a broken ankle. I worked at a church in Toronto. One night, while driving home from work, I had a strange sense to pray for protection. I prayed the entire 45-minute drive home and arrived safe. I felt relieved!

Arriving home, I began talking to my roommate—let's call her Jane. She was in a precarious position, dating a man—let's call him Peter—who physically assaulted her in our home the week prior. He demonstrated signs of addictive behaviour and presented rapid mood changes when intoxicated. Unpredictability encompassed our lives because of his addiction. I learned about the cycles of substance dependence.

The night he assaulted her was crazed. Their voices escalated, and I turned up my music in an attempt to drown out the hurtful words. I was unfamiliar with that level of rage, and I felt like a child trying to drown out their parents' arguments.

A few minutes had passed when the thought occurred to me, "What if something happens to her, and you don't hear because of the music?"

I sensed that this thought may be from God, so I turned down the music and went to the bathroom at the top of the stairs. While brushing my teeth and listening to the screaming, I heard what sounded like someone being hit, and falling. I raced down the stairs and arriving on the scene I heard them both allege that, "The other had done it." I believed her.

Jane called the police, but then hung up when he challenged her, "Do you really want to do that?"

The police called back and insisted on coming to the house. Jane sent me next door to a friend's house. As is common in domestic violence, both parties lied to the police.

When I woke up the next morning, I observed Peter and Jane calmly having breakfast in our kitchen. I was baffled. Last night this man assaulted her and today he was eating breakfast at my house like nothing happened.

The days stretched before me. What would life be like with this level of violence in our home?

We suffered instability and drama because of his addiction, now add the complexities of domestic violence. Research suggests that domestic violence is rarely an isolated incident. For me, striking a woman is a rigid boundary not to be crossed.

I advised Jane that Peter was not welcome in our home moving forward.

Ultimately, if she chose to subject herself to further abuse that was out of my control. I was, however, unwilling to risk further altercations in my home. I was trying to protect myself and save her; a mission that would ultimately end in defeat.

One of life's lessons. You can't save someone who doesn't want to be saved.

I would have laid my life down for my friend, but quickly realized there was nothing I could do.

Arriving home that night I engaged her in conversation about the impact of domestic violence and tried to validate her as undeserving of abusive behaviour.

She was not open to listening. I was trying to save her, and she was trying to save him.

Amidst the argument, I slipped on the stairs and landed hard on my ankle.

Incredible pain overwhelmed me as I noticed my ankle was facing sideways on my leg. I was horrified. An ambulance arrived shortly after my fall, and so began what I call, "My Job experience." This experience is based on the character in the Bible who loses everything, despite his faithfulness to God.

I underwent a surgical procedure to implant hardware into my ankle.

Having survived a few painful days in hospital, my parents took me to their home in Windsor. They supported me through post-surgical recovery.

Everything in my life stopped. I lay in bed wrestling with the current circumstances of my injury. I grieved for Jane, and her **presenting** mistreatment.

I prayed and processed. Until I received clarity, I needed to remove myself from that dangerous situation. I dreamt of pushing Peter because I was so angry at the abuse imposed on my best friend.

God began to show me that I had a saviour complex. He made it crystal clear that, "You can't save someone who doesn't want saving."

This thought was new. I was motivated by compassion, but I needed to learn healthy boundaries. I experienced tears and grief, but knew I had to move out of that house.

To complicate matters further, Jane and I ran a business together and co-facilitated a small church group. I realized that because she lacked healthy boundaries, she was unable to protect either of us.

I had been experiencing emotional turmoil, and financial distress as the result of Peter's addiction.

Upon returning to work, I distanced myself from my roommate. Eventually, I left the business, quit the small group and moved out. It was an incredibly painful time. I was couch hopping from my pastor's family to a co-worker's house and dependent on crutches to walk. Additionally, my employer laid me off—sort of. I was a freelance contractor, and they wanted me on staff. So, they terminated my contract on August 31st, and offered me the same position, on staff, the following day.

My challenge was an abusive work situation, inflicted by my manager. I cried myself to sleep at night due to suffering extreme levels of control–including being berated if I spent too much time in the washroom or engaged in communication with others. As the result, when first approached about coming on staff I said, "No." I felt I had established a sense of boundaries in my role as a freelance contractor and lacked peace about varying commitments. After receiving a letter outlining the termination and job offer, I submitted my resignation. I loved the ministry, but the leadership was untenable.

Unfortunately, the losses continued. I took my car in for repairs and was told the unibody was failing—it was unsafe to drive. The car was unfixable.

Struggling to survive the recent job loss, I was not able to buy a new car.

I was jobless, homeless, car-less, had lost my best friend and ministry opportunities, and I couldn't walk! '*Could life get any more challenging? Sadly, yes!*'

Unemployment left me no choice but to move in with my parents, who I hadn't lived with in over a decade. It was humiliating. As I prayerfully packed up my belongings, God began to show me that He wanted me to give my two beloved cats to my roommate. This instigated a flood of tears.

"How much more do you want to take from me God? What's left?"

To add insult to injury, people judged me for distancing myself from my friend. One individual accused me of being jealous of her relationship with Peter, and insinuated I was acting on emotions. I couldn't defend my choices without revealing details of her personal life, so I stayed silent and endured the judgement.

Moving home presented another challenge. My phone carrier was taking me to court because of unpaid long-distance charges incurred by Peter.

Unfortunately, the account was in my name, and neither Jane nor Peter had the funds to pay the bill. I had a good credit rating and litigation terrified me. The night before the bill went to collections, a long-time friend paid the bill, and refused reimbursement. It was an unforgettable act of kindness. It touches my heart to this day.

Moving home caused me to fall into a deep depression. I cried an ocean of tears.

Why would God allow incredible hardships to befall me?

I had never been so committed or passionate about following Him. '*Was this my reward?*'

I was confused and broken. According to my theology, God would reward my commitment with blessings, not hardship. My parents were wonderful, but I felt humiliated and lost.

I met three older ladies while attending a wonderful church near my parents' house. They were strong prayer warriors and I asked to join them in prayer. As we spent time together, we began to explore some of the deep wounds I'd suffered throughout my life. Deluded by the status quo of a good Christian girl, I stuffed my emotions deep within, and dissociated from the pain. I thought that negative emotions weren't Godly, and consequently, denied them. I became completely detached from my emotions. These ladies spent hours prayerfully engaging me in a deep healing process of forgiveness and identity restoration.

At the time, I lacked cognitive understanding of the healing process, and felt extremely transparent and vulnerable-like I was walking around skinless. My emotional state felt raw as I experienced the pain of my current circumstances, and the traumatic release of suppressed emotions. It was unpleasant, and God felt distant. I did, however, press forward in faith, knowing that God had orchestrated my healing journey.

In hindsight, I wouldn't have explored the depth of my emotional pain had I not felt so broken. God broke the shell that encompassed my heart.

I've learned that left to our own devices, we avoid pain at all costs. Pain was the catalyst that catapulted me on a journey to face the chains that bound my broken heart. A journey that would lay the foundation for the next decade of ministry in my life.

Working to resolve my identity crisis allowed me to recognize an unhealthy behavioural pattern of people pleasing and a lack of healthy boundaries. This would be incredibly important in my media career! I needed to learn to be authentic in my self-expression, opinions and presence. I am a 'work in process.'

I wrestled with the question, *'Why, why did God allow this to happen to me? How do I trust a God that is unpredictable and could take everything from me in the blink of an eye?'*

I didn't know how to find peace within the concept of this new version of God. I had been raised in a movement that believed God followed rules set out in scripture—if I do this, He will do that. I felt insecure and anxious outside the borders of predictability.

This wrestling continued for years as I tried to understand how to find peace along this new continuum.

In hindsight, I recognized that an answer to prayer doesn't always present within my anticipated ideals. I wanted to know the true and living God.

I had a call on my life to advocate for people who were suffering and oppressed. If I hadn't experienced God's goodness and mercy amidst suffering, then I would have lacked the ability to comfort others.

Eventually I realized that God had been preparing my heart during the months preceding my losses.

Preparation began while producing a radio show; I interviewed a woman about her experience with breast cancer. She prayed continuously for a miracle.

During her surgery the doctor could not find any previously noted lumps. She had been miraculously healed!

She quietly confessed to me that, *"My breast was mangled from the surgery."*

I told her, *"Yes, but you can be healed from that!"*

As I spoke, I felt a disquiet in my spirit. I knew what I had spoken was not from God. I was confused, *"Why not?"*

God whispered to me in response, *"Battle scars."*

He sounded incredibly proud. I didn't understand so I internalized the dialogue for future pondering.

Preparation continued as I was reviewing footage of a church service with Canadian spiritual pioneers Bill and Gwen Prankard. I admired their work in Northern Canada. As I watched the footage, I saw a spiritual impression of tire tracks over their bodies.

I asked God for clarity, and He said, "It was the price they paid to take the gospel across the nation."

Then He proudly said, *"Battle scars."*

I was starting to recognize a theme! We honour God through the price we pay for our service to Him.

God continued to prepare my heart via a church service the following week.

After the service my pastor approached me and said, *"The scars that I bear from ministry are Sergeant's stripes in the spirit."*

Then he walked away.

I was completely flabbergasted. How in the world did he know what God was talking to me about?

What prompted the pastor to say that?

As I tried to process these unusual supernatural teachings I asked God,

"What is the difference between battle scars and war wounds?"

God clearly stated,

"A war wound is a wound that hasn't healed. A battle scar is a wound that has healed and left its mark on you."

Throughout our life, we acquire scars which, paradoxically, are the place from which we minister to others.

Isaiah 61 explains that Jesus came to give us a crown of beauty for the ashes. I have witnessed this truth worldwide.

Our scars help us bring hope to others.

I've learned that during painful experiences, God is doing incredible things.

The enemy of our soul has intention for our destruction. But, as seen in the life of Jesus, when it appears like the enemy is winning, God has another plan in motion.

He will not leave us to destruction, He will restore all that we've lost. Years later, I have witnessed God restore more than I lost.

I've learned God can be orchestrating a variety of outcomes in any given situation. We may become privy to a few, but until eternity, we may never fully comprehend God's ways. This is where faith and trust come in. For years I maintained the illusion that I had control over my life. Only God knows the number of our days and what our journey will hold.

For me, when the bubble of control burst, I felt vulnerable and raw. Since then, I've learned to cling to God, even when I lack understanding. I declare His goodness over my life when everything around me seems chaotic.

Intimacy with God involves profound trust—in both our eternal salvation, and His good intentions for our life.

In hindsight, I have realized that the work he wanted to do in my heart and life was more important than my temporal comfort.

The healing I experienced during the prayer sessions laid a foundation for a decade of ministry. My response changed toward abusive leaders. I learned how to stand up for myself and others—offering complete forgiveness.

The insight gleaned about who God is in suffering has helped me advocate and comfort those experiencing crisis worldwide.

I maintain a daily awareness that, *"All I have comes from him."*

When facing your own storm, it's important to spend time seeking God, even when it appears like He is the one hurting you. His intention is never to harm. When we surrender our lives to Him, we often still question why He allows storms. It's helpful to remember times we experienced His faithfulness.

Jewish culture celebrates His faithfulness annually through festivals and celebrations. As finite humans, we need frequent reminders of God's faithfulness and kindness. We also see demonstrations of God's faithfulness through scripture. We are naturally drawn to where we focus our time and attention.

We can experience emotional exhaustion if excessively ruminating on our pain, offence, and despair. We must choose to intentionally engage hopeful thoughts and recognize we are in a spiritual battle. The battle is in our mind.

I have found worship and soaking music incredibly helpful during my bouts of grief. Music assisted me in focusing my thoughts on God and drew me close to Him.

We won't always feel intimacy with God, but we implement these tools as an act of faith.

As the host of a national Christian television show in Canada, I remind people that, *"Your today is not your forever."*

Storms can feel never ending—or unrecoverable--that is not the truth.

One of my favourite scripture verses is Psalm 30:5, *"Weeping may last through the night, but joy comes with the morning."*

I see this verse play out in my interviews with people as they share their heart wrenching stories. They were often experiencing complete despair, even considering death by suicide—but now they testify that the goodness of God transformed their life.

God promises restoration, sometimes immediately and sometimes incrementally. Restoration may manifest contrary to how we imagined, but as Psalm 27:13 says, "*We will see His goodness in the land of the living.*"

I saw that restoration happen in my own life, with a much better job, place to live, ministry opportunities and deeper trust in my Father in heaven.

I not only experienced deep healing, but also a deeper understanding of how to cling to God when I don't understand my circumstances. It has been foundational for everything that has happened in my life since that time. When I asked to know God as He genuinely is, I didn't realize that I was missing a huge piece of the puzzle. He so graciously taught me about it, and that knowledge undergirds all my advocacy for others who are suffering globally.

Friend, as you face battles, I pray that your morning comes quickly, and that God transforms the ashes of your life into a stunning crown of beauty. Because, as I've learned firsthand, that is who God is.

In His Word I Hope, Cheryl

Chapter Four

In His Word I Hope

Lisa Nigh

LAST NIGHT, I DREAMT that my mom was holding my twin daughter, Hope, lovingly in her arms. Mom had long hair and rosy cheeks, and her physique was a little plump. Speaking in Italian, she prompted me to take pictures and stated she had to go. I took numerous photos from every angle. She began to cry; she had to go.

I begged her, *"Mom, you're healthy. Please stay with me."*

It was then that I awoke.

I'm well acquainted with painful, adverse life events. I struggled with anemia, shyness, and scoliosis throughout childhood—so severe that I had to wear a body cast.

I experienced grief and loss for a beloved uncle who, at the age of 32, lost his battle with colon cancer leaving four children fatherless.

After completing university, I moved to Toronto, a 20-hour trek away. Distanced from loved ones, I determined to establish a career in the big city and begin a life with my future husband. Lacking any coping skills, I put on my big girl pants and adapted to the changes.

My family was very close-knit. The daughter of immigrants, my nana taught me how to pray with devotion—I even prayed for clear skin in my teen years.

Pregnant with our second child, we received news that I was carrying twins and that one of the twins were smaller. During my third trimester, I was confined to complete bed rest due to experiencing pre-term labour at 20 weeks.

My mom stayed with us, offering support and care for our three-year-old daughter. Mom was by my side for every major life event.

When the twins were born, mom's catholic ambition was to have them baptized in the hospital. She was the last one to hold Hope alive. Losing a child was painful beyond comprehension or words. I prayed, asking God, "To hold my daughter alive."

I held her close to my heart for one hour.

I prayed that her twin brother would be healthy, and by God's grace, our son was given a clean bill of health.

Years later, my father was feeling unwell, and I flew to be with him in Thunder Bay. I was by his side as he endured a litany of medical tests. We were devastated to learn that, at 68 years of age, he had stage four pancreatic cancer. Dad's wish was to die at home, so I moved home to help with his care. Together we coped with the finite reality of his life. I prayed daily for his pain to be managed. I prayed for clarity and a deflated ego regarding necessary decision-making.

Dad lived for three months and passed peacefully in 2017.

My mind, body, and soul were catapulted into a state of shock and survival. My ego was set aside for three months. I was no longer a wife, mother, or daughter. I was the caretaker of dad's walk to 'the pearly gates.'

I was grateful for the love and support of my husband and children. They flew home regularly to support us. It was such an ugly time. I adapted. I prayed.

The days following dad's death were surreal; it took years to recall the tragic effects of grief and loss.

Fast forward to the Covid pandemic, a story that has changed me.

All the mountains strewn before me prepared me to walk through Covid calmly. I am a realist.

After dad passed, my mom suffered a broken heart and came to live with us for ten months. With the help of an astute team of doctors and nurses, we supported her physical and emotional needs, including acute care after knee surgery. We helped break her dependency on sleeping pills. Her vitality returned, and she yearned to go home.

Within a few years, my mom's health began to deteriorate. In the winter of 2021, she was diagnosed with acute pneumonia and was admitted to the hospital. In May of 2022, her health took a turn for the worse, and she was rushed to the hospital. I maintained continual contact to ensure her well-being.

On one occasion, I spoke with her in the morning, and she became critically ill with a mysterious health issue by evening. I insisted mom be flown to a critical care center. Covid restrictions hindered my ability to attend a flight to be by her side. Upon receiving assurance from the medical team that mom's condition had stabilized, I confirmed I would drive to the care center the following Monday.

At 3:00 a.m. the next day, I was informed her condition was critical and initiated travel arrangements immediately.

My heart stopped!

I booked a flight for 8:00 a.m. and arrived at the airport accordingly. As I was boarding the plane, my phone rang. The caller said, *"Lisa are you sitting down? Your mom has passed."*

I was robbed of the opportunity to be with my mom in her time of need. I was heartbroken beyond measure. I cried violently for one and a half hours.

My mom's body lay lifeless before me; beautifully dainty—little hands, arthritic feet, and kept hair. I soaked in the essence of her presence. I cyclically ruminated on reels of memories. I felt like an orphan.

'I spoke with my mom every day of my life. Now what?'

Covid prevented our family from gathering. Despite the painfully small funeral size, I gleaned a sense of peace, knowing mom was in heaven.

She was faithful and personable. She was kinder to people than they deserved. My mom lived a humble, cautious and gentle life. She listened and loved without condition.

'I endured hardships in life with my mom by my side. How was I going to handle her death without her?'

It was months before my anger subsided before I could embrace sleep without visualizing her face amidst a fountain of tears. Her mom-isms played their narrative in my life through my family.

As I reflect, I realize how blessed I was to have a mom who was *FOR* me. I cherish how I felt in her presence. During the past nine months, I have learned of the numerous people gifted by her company.

The sadness in life has been a catalyst propelling me to amplify her grace, to seize the opportunity of allowing, '*her ceiling to present my floor.*'

My daughter's headstone reads,

"I wait for the Lord, my soul waits, and in His Word, I hope."

May the grace of the Lord, which surpasses understanding, be with you all.

Love, Lisa

Chapter Five

Some Rainbows Take Time

Rachelle Van Ryssen

AS A CHILD OF the seventies, I, like many in my age group remember a simpler time and for me, it was a time of growth and wonder. As a kid with an enormous imagination, I examined every experience as an opportunity to create adventurous stories for each mundane event of my young life.

I was able to imagine magical scenarios in ordinary daily routines.

I grew up with my parents and sister, Janet, in a little bayside community called, St. Williams.

My dad, who was born in Montreal, worked installing drywall and as a commercial fisherman in Booth Harbour on Lake Erie.

He was an entertaining storyteller and had me envisioning pirates, battles with sea monsters, and enormous waves that would envelop my dad's boat! Thankfully, that wasn't the case!

We lived in a century-old house. It was a quaint, white, two-story, wooden home with green shutters and a lovely front porch. The house was surrounded by flowering bushes and was well maintained. My favourite was a forsythia tree in the spring it was lush and full of yellow blooms.

Although attractive, functionally the house had single pane windows and was heated by a lone, Franklin wood stove on the main floor. It was cold in the winter. The house would cry out with creaks, cracks, and moans against fierce winter blizzards and the unforgiving winds of summer.

Thunderstorms rolled off Lake Erie and the wheat field in front of our house.

On stormy nights while tucking myself into bed, I would worry that a blustering wind would blow the house over like the story of the "Three Little Pigs." Leaving my home in a pile of sticks!

I both respected and feared the strength of storms, feeling blessed when they passed.

In the post-storm moments, I exhaled and visualized the storm dissipating. I imagined that it was sucked up into the atmosphere like an enormous vacuum had appeared from heaven.

I then would resume my adventures as though the storm had been a figment of my vivid imagination.

I recall attending Sunday school at a small wooden Baptist church in St. Williams. My dad taught a group of kids from the tiny village.

Dad shared the story of how Jesus calmed the storm! Unbeknownst to me at the time, that story became deeply rooted.

To this day I am fascinated with the power of large storms. Storms that tear across the Great Lakes, so mighty, frightening and exhilarating—they have never disappointed!

Through the years, I became aware that, although powerful, a storm's power is no match for the power of the Creator.

Despite their magnitude, storms don't last forever. Best of all, the One [Jesus] who speaks to storms can cause them to stop with a word.

Mark 4:35-41 **Jesus Calms the Storm**

35 *That day when evening came, he said to his disciples, "Let us go over to the other side."* ***36*** *Leaving the crowd behind, they took him along, just as he was, in the boat. There were also other boats with him.*

37 *A furious squall came up, and the waves broke over the boat, so that it was nearly swamped.*

38 *Jesus was in the stern, sleeping on a cushion. The disciples woke him and said to him, "Teacher, don't you care if we drown?"*

39 *He got up, rebuked the wind and said to the waves, "Quiet! Be still!" Then the wind died down and it was completely calm.*

40 *He said to his disciples, "Why are you so afraid? Do you still have no faith?"*

41 *They were terrified and asked each other, "Who is this? Even the wind and the waves obey him!"*

About a year ago my husband, John and I drove to Port Dover a small port town on Lake Erie, to watch a thunderstorm roll in. We drove through hail and rain and watched as the sunlight pressed through the dark— dividing the sky from the clouds. It looked like a painting of Heaven breaking through a darkened canvas.

Golden rays burst through, birthing a gorgeous blue sky. In the distance, a rainbow appeared with amazing vibrancy amidst the cerulean sky.

A few minutes later a second rainbow appeared above the first. As we drove, rainbows surrounded us. I casually said to John, "*We have always been, "storm chasers," haven't we? Today we are chasing rainbows.*"

He smiled in agreement. I smiled and thought, we are rainbow chasers. Wow, that would be an excellent name for a book! And so, "Chasing Rainbows," was conceived.

Over the next few weeks God placed the names of thirteen women in my heart. Most were women I knew personally; a few were recommended — all the women were connected in some way.

I engaged them through FaceTime and Zoom calls and fell in love with their stories. I embraced a knowing that God sent each woman to join me in compiling a commission by God.

I was '*however*' surprised by the direction that God presented for my personal chapter. As an author of several books, my readers may conclude that my storms would tell of life's traumas. My husband's heart attack and related heart surgery, the difficult birthing of my son and his journey with Asperger's, watching my daughter face anxiety, holding my best friend's face as she`died in my hands or the litany of physical battles I have endured.

The systemic effects of Multiple Sclerosis presented a need to relearn how to walk—not once but three times. A brain bleed rendered me unable to recognize my children and husband.

Recovery from fear envelops families living with a loved one who suffers chronic illness—being admitted to the hospital for over a month and struggling with the uncertainty of a life-or-death prognosis. '*All while recognizing that life carries on without me!?*'

How about the brain tumour in my right temporal lobe that has caused memory issues?

Nope!

Indeed, He would have me write about the story of being a cancer survivor?

Nope!

These were not the storms God wanted me to share!

I felt confused.

As I read the stories of the other rainbow chasers in this book, I learned that their experiences encompassed most of my storms and more.

So, I had to spend time with God in prayer. I hit empty—a blank slate. I surrendered, let go, and gave it to God.

Then came my *'aha!'* moment. The one storm that continually blows into my life like a hurricane is *other people's opinions*— my need for them and how to deal with them righteously.

Some of you may think, that is ridiculous!

How can someone who has lived through so much be shaken by what others say about them?

Well, quite frankly, the thorn in my flesh is pride.

I love my family deeply. We are in a beautiful place. But life wasn't always wonderful.

I was raised in an alcoholic home. I sometimes felt as though a bottle of alcohol had far more worth than, me. I held to this belief and knew it to be true because when I cried and begged my family member to stop drinking, they yelled and said, *"No."*

They would send me away and grab their bottle of booze.

The fight for their sobriety was an argument that would trigger a fountain of tears and continued for years. I can happily report that drinking is no longer an issue in our family and fences have been mended. But for a time, some wounds remained.

So, the same little girl whose imagination could touch the stars, who played the role of a peacemaker, who was tender-hearted and cherished Jesus became a people pleaser, a joker, and an expert manipulator just to emotionally survive.

At the age of 30, I faced a choice. I was diagnosed with Multiple Sclerosis and a short time later a brain tumour. I could have chosen to let a diagnosis ruin my life or in my mind I thought I could embrace it as a platform to demonstrate my worth—I convinced myself that I was stronger than this illness.

I was blessed to be surrounded by big-hearted people who supported my family. I was amazed at the kindness, love, and transparency of others. If I am honest, I sponged up the attention. I mistook attention for love. I became an attention whore.

It took time to recognize the attention-seeking behaviour and shift to a God focused and a Jesus filtered life.

My identity became lost beneath the facade of a perpetually cheerful, witty woman with Multiple Sclerosis! I have even since learned of a condition called smiling depression.

People introduced me to their friends, as "*their friend, Rachelle, you know the one with MS.*"

I wanted to make people happy and had an innate need to belong; I desired to be everyone's favourite.

When you feel less than in childhood, you will find yourself looking to fill the void as an adult.

Despite having a husband who adored me and a loving family, I felt like a damaged child longing to hear that I was loved, more than a bottle of alcohol. I needed to be worth more than an addiction to a substance. I needed to feel loved and cherished. I wanted to feel important.

As written by fellow Rainbow Chaser, Karen deBlieck, I recall the childhood terror of being chosen last for sports picks. So, as a child, I became a first-pick athlete, yet my heart still shuddered during the team selection process. I knew that much of the process was based on popularity. Despite the frequency of being chosen in the top three picks, my heart anxiously vibrated until they called my name.

As an adult in my early thirties, I still required praise. I attained it by becoming an inspirational speaker and author. I even studied theology and was ordained. I coveted acceptance and needed to feel worthy. I collected people who found me praiseworthy and inspiring. I needed people to prop me up, who adored my fantastic attitude.

I maintained a good sense of humour and have been gifted with a contagious wit. I controlled the narrative through humour to deflect people from closeness or possible interrogation. *'if they truly knew me, they would figure out that I was a fraud! My heart was broken, I was terribly afraid and sometimes when I was preaching, I was also wondering if what I was teaching was true?'*

If I could keep people laughing, I was in control.

I developed dysfunctional thinking patterns and deflection skills.

My lifestyle became counterintuitive to the likeness of Christ. As my earthly status grew, *mostly in my own mind.* I drifted further from God—the same God who walked me through hard times and calmed the storms in my life. I preached about Him, I taught about and wrote about Him all the while becoming my own god.

It is often noted that God has a sense of humour. The same God that created the world loved me enough to place a narcissist in my life. Wow! Talk about a way to make a person review their own behaviour. This narcissist was so manipulative that I spun out of control, trying to keep them happy. In time, I realized they mirrored some of the defects that were out of alignment in my own life.

Without God in my life, I would have continued to exhibit narcissistic tendencies perhaps even fully becoming a Narcissist completely.

I prayed, I repented, and pleaded with Jesus to help me. I didn't know what to pray but I was confident that God knew what I needed.

The Lord dealt with my pride and ego. He stripped the hardened callus that encased my heart. *'The callus that once protected a little girl was now hurting the woman. It was stopping me from flourishing, from feeling, loving and truly being loved.'*

As I learned to relinquish my life to Him, my heart grew increasingly sensitive. I could see everyone through the eyes of Jesus. I was filled with compassion and love.

I overflowed with joy and peace—the peace that passes all understanding. Philippians 4:7, *And the peace of God, which transcends all understanding, will guard your hearts and your minds in Christ Jesus.*

I sought opportunities to forgive and love on people!

The more I surrendered myself to Jesus and deflated my ego the more God filled me.

I have observed authentic beauty in all my relationships, and God holds me safely in His presence—I want for nothing. I am loved and cherished. God overwhelms me with an abundance of love and divine friendships.

I still backslide and battle the ability to share how I am feeling authentically. I default to humour and at times divert the conversation when feeling uncomfortable discussing health issues. But I too am a work in progress!

I value my God given ability to express joy and laughter.

I am still, at times, reluctant to trust human sincerity and wonder whether people truly care about my well-being? But I no longer meditate on that way of thinking. Instead, I take solace in the knowledge that God is with me. I have all that I will ever need. He is all the love and acceptance any of us need.

As a Christian woman in her 50s, I have surpassed milestones that I never thought I would live to see. I have authentic friendships and intimate relationships with my family. I maintain an enduring love with my husband, John, and we have grown in the Lord beyond my wildest dreams.

God has created in me the ability to build excellent relationships with my kids and friends. He gets me! My relationship with Him has taught me that a full heart requires a continual outpouring of love to others. I give Him, all of me, the good, bad, and ugly; I give it all to Him. He turns it all into beauty. As my friend, Wendy Noll, shares in her book "Ashes to Beauty!"

I am confident in my friendship with Jesus. I still have much to learn. I desire to change to glorify my Saviour. I am grateful that He is patient and loving.

Recently my faith was tested again. I set daily intentions to demonstrate Christ as laid out in biblical teaching, but due to human frailty, I fell short. I set myself up through unrealistic expectations. I outwardly presented what I felt the world wanted to see, strength, composure, and encouragement. I avoided discussing personal struggles about physical, emotional, or spiritual issues. I smiled.

However, the word of God is faithful and living; it is never changing and always perfect. We are not perfect! We are human. Once again, God has presented lessons that have taught me to let go and let God.

By allowing myself to ask for help and letting my friends know what I was dealing with I was able to get back on track! Sometimes the hands and ears God uses to help us are human.

I give myself permission to laugh, cry and live life to the fullest. I want to know God and rest in Him.

Today, I cry out to God in times of need and acknowledge that I am precious to Him.

I no longer fear storms, they remind me that a shift is about to take place. A cleansing, a time to reflect and rebuild. Storms come to bring change and rainbows come to bring promises and hope. I choose to chase the rainbow. But to experience the beauty of the rainbow we must suffer through the storm.

So put on your faith like a raincoat and trust in the One who both creates and calms the storm with a word. He will stand in the storm with you, He will calm you during the storm, and when the time is right, He will reward you with your rainbow.

P.S. Having completed my chapter, and read the chapters written by the contributing authors, God continues to reveal His presence. God highlights His connections with each of the women in this book and our connections to one another. I know He will do the same for you! Seek all of the connections as you read these stories! It is amazing!

'Please don't miss out on the lessons in the storms! And always take time to enjoy the rainbows!

In God's true love, Rachelle Van Ryssen

Chapter Six

Rainbows During COVID

Beverly Hadland

EVEN BEFORE I BECAME a Christ follower, on October 13, 1981, I always chased rainbows. I paused in fascination and smiled every time I saw one. Rainbows reminded me of hope. They caused me to believe my painful childhood memories had purpose and meaning.

Being hurt by several influential Christians did not stop me from believing in God, but it did stop me from believing in their God. I knew there had to be a higher power holding this universe together. I made the typical mistake of thinking the Creator was too busy to be concerned with someone like me.

Within weeks of my conversion, I found myself searching for a mission. God's scripture became my motto: "Seek His

Kingdom, His righteousness, and all these things will be added unto you."

God's word confirmed He had a purpose for my life. I believed God would add anything I dreamed of as I worked on His assigned missions. I didn't need to worry about it or expend energy chasing it. I needed to go about God's business. The rest would happen organically.

Over my decades with Jesus, I wrote three books, one a national best seller. I travelled the world speaking to over three million people about 'Sex, Love, and Dating.'

In 2015, God told me to close my charity and work full-time at Crossroads. It wasn't easy closing the ministry I started in the '80s. It was my baby. But I know that when God closes one door, He opens another. There would be a rainbow over the new venture because it was God's mission.

Within a few years of following God's leading, I became Crossroads Ambassador to the First People in Canada.

I've travelled His path many times, visiting sixty-three Indigenous communities and establishing loving relationships with over 100 communities. The experience has been pure joy.

At the beginning of 2020, I met with Crossroads' Indigenous T.V. producer. We planned six trips across Canada from B.C. to Nova Scotia, including attendance at the North American Indigenous Games in July.

Two days before a March mission trip to Thunder Bay, COVID hit Canada. Everything not considered by the government to be essential services shut down. The world stopped.

For the first time in history, every church, mosque, and synagogue were closed for two weeks to 'flatten the curve.' Or so we thought.

One month passed with no returning freedoms in sight. That was when Zoom meetings took off. Praise God that getting food to the Indigenous communities was a priority for the federal government. Unfortunately, outside of essentials, there was no money for indoor/outdoor activity items, books, puzzles, or crafts and no money for spiritual materials.

Communities suffered the highest drug overdoses, leading to death, massive depression, and suicide.

I was looking for the rainbow, and God came through.

During the two-year COVID lockdown, we reached out to our national partners—Canadian Bible Society, Gideons (ShareWord Canada), Life Light Ministries, Joyce Meyer Ministries, Family Life Ministries, Socks for Souls, Top Shelf Sports Equipment, and Crossroads. We shipped over one million dollars' worth of donated items to feed these isolated communities' hearts and souls. The shipping cost was $60,000.

One hundred and twenty-two Indigenous communities were impacted for good, but a desperate need still existed.

They were asking, *"Can you come? Can you visit?"*

The loneliness and the isolation were taking a toll. Many communities have no churches. No ministries could visit them due to the constant lockdowns, high COVID numbers, and fear of travel. Fear replaced faith.

During that first summer of COVID (2020), we saw things open, especially for outdoor events. Though small, it was a slight improvement over a total shutdown. Most Indigenous communities were closed off to outsiders.

Six Indigenous communities along the Alaska Highway in northern B.C. begged me to come with a prayer team. I said, *"Yes. I'll come."*

A couple from Family Life Ministries wanted to join me. Another rainbow from God.

The hardest part was wearing a mask for thirteen hours until I was outside the airport at Fort St. John. Our small team of three visited Doig River, Saulteaux, Blueberry River,

Halfway, Prophet, and Fort Nelson First Nations. We met with those who wanted prayer.

When we arrived at Halfway River Health Unit, several young people, arms wide open, came running towards us for hugs and attention. No fear at all. They were so happy that someone cared enough to come and bless them.

That's all we did. We rejected fear. We showed up with food; we listened, hugged, and prayed for each person who came to the centre. Volunteers brought elders for prayer who had not left their homes in months. It was amazing.

As I finished praying for an elder, a phone was placed in my hand. Chief Darlene Hunter wanted to speak with me. She was sorry she couldn't be there to thank us in person. Chief Hunter had buried fourteen people in the last fourteen weeks. Not one from COVID.

They were seeing a 93% increase in suicides compared to 2019. The Chief's community was overwhelmed with grief, numb with the pain... and isolation. Chief Darlene was grateful for our visit. She said, *"It gave her hope for the future."*

Another rainbow from God. Another, but not the last.

God showed me a rainbow would open for me to take a team across Canada, in an R.V., from July 17 to August 8, 2021. We had to travel on those dates, and it had to be in an R.V.

Honestly, the trip did not look encouraging. Lockdowns continued across Canada the entire year, even into the spring of 2022. Planning had to start in the fall of 2021 with Crossroads still under a 'no travel ban.' I had no doubt and no fear. We had to go through with the planning--trusting and believing God would make a way.

It was nine months of preparing, planning meetings, waiting on God for His team selection, and satisfying all COVID travel mandates and protocols.

Most Canadians would not believe this was possible. I must be dreaming or chasing a rainbow!!!

God kept telling me to focus on His light and His mission. He formed a team consisting of Metis, Taino, Mohawk, Cree, and me (Heinz 57, as they say). We met on Zoom for three months and only met in person the day we began our trip.

Each team member had to isolate themselves for two weeks before the in-person meeting. Before our first meal together, we monitored our temperatures and filled out COVID forms.

However, once that was completed, we became instant family.

I loved what God was doing. Five women from five nations, travelling across five provinces to re-ignite hope among the Indigenous communities.

When God says to do something, we can have confidence it will happen no matter how it appears in the natural realm.

What an exercise in faith over fear.

This planning happened long before discovering the missing children at Kamloops Indian Residential School. God knew this would be revealed to the world in May of 2021. And there we were, ready to visit the nine communities who extended invitations and spend the August long weekend in Kamloops—including a special visit to the residential school.

Enforced lockdowns and travel bans were in place until the day we left, July 17. People told us we were crazy. How could we travel west not knowing if travel bans would be lifted in time?

We drove across Ontario overnighting in campgrounds during the lockdown. No washrooms were open but praise God; we had ours in the R.V. Restaurants offered outdoor patios and takeout. Manitoba was still under lockdown, so we could only drive across the province on the main highway.

With no campgrounds open, we drove straight through Manitoba to Saskatchewan.

On July 20, the day we arrived at camp, mask and social distancing mandates were lifted. All signs of COVID were gone. It felt like being in another country. Praise God. Freedom. Another rainbow.

Our team began the ten-hour drive to Birch Narrows—Turnor Lake. On arrival, we unloaded large gift bowls of food and snacks for the forty-nine community elders. It was their first gathering at the community kitchen since COVID upended their lives.

What a fantastic start to our trip.

After three days, we set out to Ministikwan First Nation Bible Camp. Our mission was to help clean the kitchen as the camp prepared to open for the first time since COVID shut down the world.

First to arrive, our task was to pray over the property, cabins, kitchen, and chapel. Twenty leaders came shortly after our arrival. Our next mission was apparent, cook great meals. It was a beautiful exchange of hard work, fellowship, worship, and prayer over the young leaders.

During the trip, I found it profound that every community we visited had utterly stopped living due to COVID. Our appearance re-ignited hope and energy among the Indigenous communities.

Our third stop was Onion Lake Cree Nation church and food bank. Our team helped the congregation prepare their first community meal since the onset of COVID. We led the church service with our testimonies and prayers. I wasn't surprised that no one had ever seen a Taino Indigenous person—one of the team members. The Taino Indigenous people were the first to encounter Christopher Columbus in 1492.

Our team was invited to a prayer walk at two residential school sites—sites that were being prepared for radar machines that would scan the land. The procedure is very sacred to the community; we humbly recognized the honour and privilege as we walked in prayer on this sacred land.

Our following invitation was to Big Island First Nation. In the past, we ministered with Pastor Ann Bear in the church located on the reserve. This time, the Chief offered us the community centre and invited the people to come for prayer. Dozens of men, women, and youth, including the Chief and his wife, were grateful someone came to pray and encourage their people.

Our last Saskatchewan community was Thunderchild Cree Nation. Again, the Chief asked Pastor Alvina if we would come to the band office and pray for his staff.

The office was overwhelmed with grief at the sudden loss of three staff members within one week. We could feel the pain and suffering. Our team went from office to office and room to room. All but one staff member accepted prayer.

They were grateful for our prayers and fellowship. We felt spent but pleased about the ministry engagements by day's end. Few would remember our names, but they would never forget that five women from five nations travelled in an R.V. to provide encouragement and prayers.

During the next several days, we visited communities in Alberta. We took a day off to relax and prepare for our final destination, Kamloops Indian Residential School.

Over six hundred fires raged in British Columbia; some were fifteen kilometres from our destination. While authorities did not order us to leave, they were discouraging travel.

We received phone calls, texts, and emails with the same concerns.

"DO NOT GO TO BC, RETURN HOME."

We couldn't return home. We were on God's mission. Not one of our team felt we were to turn back. Each felt called by GOD. We were like Debra in the Bible, chomping at the bit to bring their regalia, language, culture, and traditions together under the love of Jesus.

After prayer and confirmation from God, the entire team agreed we would drive until we were blocked.

I called ahead to confirm our rooms. The hotel was located across the river from the residential school. The Muslim staff heard of our tour. We later learned they were excited to meet the HOPE team.

We spent three nights in that hotel, each of us pleased to have our own bed and long morning showers. Another team member and I were the designated drivers for the 10,638 KM trip. Imagine how thankful we were to park the R.V. and relax in our rooms.

Understandably, money is frequently a sticking point. Praise God: we raised sufficient funds for the trip and to cover travel costs for twenty-eight Indigenous People—many of whom were residential school survivors and their families. They felt blessed to make the pilgrimage to Kamloops and share our lodging and fellowship.

The staff let us gather on the back patio for a meet and greet—a spontaneous time of prayers and blessings.

Indigenous people flew in from Ontario and travelled by car from Manitoba, Saskatchewan, Alberta, and northern B.C., Dene, Beaver, Cree, Ojibwe, and Metis. They met for the first time, offering solidarity and support. Several residential school survivors shared their journey of pain. Their adult children and grandchildren heard unfortunate truths for the first time—a time of healing was had by many.

The next day, this group of Indigenous people trekked across the bridge to the Kamloops Indian Residential School. Each wore their unique regalia according to their culture and traditions. One individual made baby moccasins to be buried in the orchard where the missing ones were located.

The world was aghast at the announcement—the remains of 215 children were found in an orchard at the largest residential school in Canada.

This was not a cemetery--but an orchard.

Children who died at the school, whether from illnesses, suicide or beatings, were not sent home to their families. Our Canadian government would not reimburse the school for the cost of returning the bodies.

The cheapest way to handle the burial was to wrap each body in a blanket and bury them under the trees. You may have seen news reports showing 215 little red flags marking the sites.

One might say it's hard to visualize a rainbow over this school or this historic tragedy. But there is one.

Our guide, Ted, explained that they never planned to find the missing, but it was Creator's time for the world to know. He shared that, ten years ago, an archaeological class from Fraser University asked to do a careful dig in the orchard. They heard stories suggesting remains were buried there. Students spent one semester searching the orchard. They did not find any remains but, in hindsight, learned they were only a few feet away from one of the remains.

Sometime later, the school, now a museum, received a significant donation to design a large garden and pathway through the orchard. But COVID made supplies challenging to secure.

An elder, who attended that school, believed her sister was buried there. Instead, she asked if the money could pay for a radar machine to attempt to *'locate the missing.'* The Indigenous do not call them bodies. The donor agreed to the request.

The radar machines finished their work on May 27. On Friday, May 28, 2021, Chief Rosanne Casimir announced the findings to the world. This was the first historical proof that there were thousands of residential school survivors whose stories were not previously believed—now they were.

The world gasped in shock. Canadians paused to reflect on the veracity of the history they were taught in schools.

This acknowledgment was symbolic of the rainbow in the sky. It seemed God was saying, *'Now it is time to face the truth, admit guilt, repent, and seek forgiveness from the First Peoples of the land.'*

Our group was the first invited to walk the orchard where the 215 missing remain buried. We were each forever changed. The next day we gathered to share, cry and pray for one another before they returned to their communities.

Manitoba was still closed. That necessitated driving straight across the province into Ontario with no stops. Ontario was still mask mandated and social distancing. It seemed the rainbow had disappeared. One could sense deep-rooted fear in people. It saddened me that half the country walked in freedom while the other half walked in fear, but that was our experience.

Life presents us with a litany of choices. I choose to look for the rainbow in every situation. I decide to walk in perfect love, which is devoid of fear. I choose to walk in faith despite presenting circumstances.

Even today, with rumours of wars, famines, earthquakes, climate change, and . . . fill in the blank. Some are way beyond rumour, as we know.

The Bible tells us these things will happen, and happening they are.

No matter what is going on, reject fear. Choose love over fear. Choose to chase the rainbows.

With love Beverly

Here is a short video of our trip. Twenty-one days in eight minutes.

https://www.youtube.com/watch?v=xrWfB3Oip-8&t=59s

Chapter Seven

My Storm Has a Name

Michelle Sim

MY STORM ARRIVED FOUR minutes after midnight on April 2, 1971. We named him James 'Paul' Sim. He was our second-born, another beautiful boy. I was 22 years old. I was unaware that this little boy would allow me to realize unimaginable intrinsic strength. Any challenge that came along over the next 51 years was, in comparison, nothing but a windy day.

I grew up in a typical family in the '50s and '60s—an early Baby Boomer. I was the middle child in a family struggling to overcome the residue of the Second World War. My dad, a handsome man of Polish descent, had not been blessed with an education. He was a hard worker and, although we had no extras, we were always well-fed, housed and loved. My mom, a fun-loving woman of English descent, greeted life with a radiant smile. She was affectionate, creative, social and actively engaged with her five children.

When I was eleven, we moved from Toronto, north, to a village of 700 people. Due to a lack of available housing in the village, we resided in an old vacant farmhouse located amidst a maze of country roads three miles out of town. I loved it.

Everything came easy to me. I was an eager student, attractive, talented, athletic, well-liked and personable. Impoverished circumstances made it necessary for me to seek employment at the age of twelve.

I engaged a variety of employment opportunities from babysitting and waitressing to pruning Christmas trees, painting lawn signs, and sitting with the elderly. During the summer months I worked full-time at a girl's camp, and part-time with my dad at his house-painting business. Employment was the only way I could acquire money. I developed a great work ethic. We were never given an allowance; however, our home life was blessed with terrific food, love and encouragement. Church life was a mainstay in most family's lives at that time.

In that village I met Ian; my now husband of 54 years. He was a rich kid. His folks had a canary yellow Corvair which Ian abused every weekend. Although brilliant, Ian hated school and failed grades several times. I came to learn that the muscled, alpha male's home life was neither secure nor happy.

We married on May 19, 1968, clueless as to what we were doing. Ian was a rookie at the Etobicoke Fire Department. We settled into an apartment close to the Firehall. Four months later, our first son Michael was born. I was more of a tomboy, so motherhood was not on my radar—until it was *(laughing out loud*). I knew nothing about caring for a newborn. Thankfully, maternal instinct kicked in.

As it turned out, Michael was the perfect little guy. At one month of age, Michael was sleeping through the night. He was keenly intelligent, reciting his alphabet at 15 months of age. He maintained a hilarious sense of humour and became my best friend. Michael's easy-going personality and unusual intellect set an unrealistic precedence that having kids was the easiest job in the world.

It didn't matter that Ian was a workaholic, nor that I was a classic co-dependent. It didn't matter that Ian worked day and night to provide for us. It didn't matter that Ian forgot that I was a nice person and was often too tired to show any appreciation.

So, it was in this blinded state we thought it was a great idea to have another child. And that brings us to April 2, 1971.

Paul, in his infancy, slept a lot and was often congested. He knew many words before the age of one and, like his older brother, was running around by 11 months. Paul had an urgency to suck and would fall asleep with two middle fingers in his mouth, and '*Peter-Pointer*' on his nose. Notably, his eyes were often puffy, and he had severe skin allergies. At the age of one, Paul was rushed to Sick Children's Hospital in Toronto because he couldn't breathe.

Paul was dangerously active, accident-prone and always running away.

We bought our first house in a quiet neighbourhood just before he was born. I spent many hours looking for and chasing after Paul. He consumed most of my waking hours, leaving little time for his brother, Ian or my, ever-increasing, emotional needs.

While playing with other children in our neighbourhood, Paul would experience frustration when trying to communicate. Although he had many words, he struggled to articulate words into understandable phrases. The result was, on average, 10 to 12 violent temper tantrums every day.

My storm was turning into a series of typhoons, leaving wakes of wreckage in their path.

In frustration, Paul stopped trying to communicate and fell behind in his development.

By the time he was four, a psychologist had referred Paul to a school for "Emotionally Disturbed Children." I was a bit distraught, to say the least, with the chosen wordage posted on a sign at the main entrance to the school. Due to daily commutes to Paul's school, we purchased a second car and I had to wait in the city until he finished his half-day class. I had no life, yet I was determined to do everything possible to help my suffering, tortured child. I love him with all my heart, then and now.

Year two at this specialized school brought Paul to the age of attending kindergarten locally. He and I would drive to Toronto in the morning. I would remain in Toronto until Paul finished his morning classes, then I would rush home to prepare lunch for both boys. After lunch I walked them back to school—just under a mile away. Our Old English Sheepdog, Fergus, would join us. Multitasking became one of my many talents.

Paul failed kindergarten and was transferred to another school in Oakville to repeat the grade. Forty years later, Paul disclosed to us that as a seven-year-old, he had been sexually assaulted in a bathroom stall while on a school trip. It's no wonder my little boy was enraged.

Lack of disclosure about the assault left us confused, disheartened and exhausted as we tried everything to help our son. We considered selling our home and sending him to a facility in Maine where he could get round-the-clock care. Moments prior to finalizing intake, a doctor revealed that there were allegations of abuse at the facility. Thank God we didn't proceed as planned.

When Paul was ten, he attended a private school in Oakville that specialized in helping children with learning disabilities. Class sizes consisted of eight students, and we received government funding to assist with costs. It was a reputable school, and he thrived there. He managed to take the town bus on his own and developed social skills which enabled him to develop friendships. With both my sons in school full-time, I found a job at a lighting store selling high-end light fixtures, designed for custom-built luxury homes.

Things were going relatively smoothly. Ian obtained both his Real Estate and Broker Licenses so he could help run his family's real estate business while his father recovered from back-to-back heart surgeries. With a natural talent for real-estate, Ian was putting in long hours up north at the family business. He would return home when on shift at the Fire Department. Ian was often away from home for extended periods of time due to a busy work life. I tended to the kids with all their needs, cared for the animals and worked full-time. I barely survived the various household chores--cleaning, cooking, laundry, shopping, paying bills, and chauffeuring. I managed but there was significant stress on our marriage.

Then, in 1981 life presented an ugly, relentless recession. Ian had been working on a real estate deal that, had it worked out, would have placed us in a beautiful, new, mortgage-free home. What started as a great intention, took a turn for the worse, and we got stuck with two houses—unable to sell either one. Mortgage rates had risen to 20%, construction stopped, real estate sales plummeted, and people stopped buying high-end light fixtures.

We now had two houses and half the income. We also lost our funding for Paul's schooling and had to find an alternative source. We were in a messs – both financially and personally. The boys could sense something was wrong. My older son was managing, but Paul was acting out. The level of stress in our home was suffocating.

One of my customers at the lighting store was Ruth Zammit. Most customers were miserable due to the recession, but not Ruth. Ruth was peaceful, kind, happy and never fazed about backorders. There was something different about Ruth. One day she asked me to stop by her new home to see the installed light fixtures.

Her home was peaceful and decorated with elegance. Most walls were decorated with, what I called at the time, 'God-plaques.' Jesus 'this' and Jesus' that.'

I couldn't help but ask, *"Ruth! What the hell are all these God-plaques?"* (Oh boy, Michelle!)

Ruth so patiently replied, *"Oh Michelle, Jesus is my best friend."*

"Oh, that's nice Ruth," I said, trying to mask my sarcasm.

Ruth was unaware that I was struggling with being overcome by depression. To appease Ruth as a customer, I let her tell me a little about Jesus. I told Ruth about the financial trouble we were in, and she said she would pray for me.

A couple of months went by, and the deal was about to close on the second home we had purchased. Ian and I were panicking about our situation. Ruth called regularly to ask how I was doing. I was always polite, but frankly, I didn't know what to say.

One day, compelled to call Ruth, I said, *"Ruth, you aren't praying hard enough because we are in a mess, and nothing is happening. I don't know what to do."*

Her soothing voice replied, *"You have to pray Michelle."*

As I recalled fond memories of childhood days at the Anglican Church I replied,

"I don't know how to pray Ruth; I lost my Prayer Book years ago."

"Just talk to God, Michelle. You don't need a Prayer Book. Just tell Him how you are feeling. He'll hear you and answer you," she said.

To say, I was *ticked*, is an understatement! I didn't need to *'talk to God.'* I needed out of my situation! I needed someone to help me before I completely fell apart under the strain of life. PRAY?

I said, *"Thank you, Ruth,"* and hung up the phone.

A couple of months passed, and the deal on the second house closed. I was depressed and losing my peripheral vision. Everyone in our household was acting out.

On the morning of February 22, 1982, in a state of desperation and alone in the house, I had fallen asleep at the kitchen table with my head resting on an empty coffee mug. When I woke up, I went to the washroom and looked in the mirror. The coffee mug had left an imprint on my forehead. I looked horrid. Then, unmistakably I heard,

"Michelle, you have to pray. Just talk to God."

How does one describe a *Holy thing*?

A Loving Force drew me up to my bedroom, where I fell on my knees and cried out to a God—who I no longer believed existed. I poured my heart out to Him. I told Him I couldn't go on like this anymore. I didn't want to be like this. I wanted to love my family.

"Please help me. IF YOU EXIST, HELP ME!"

I can't recall how long I remained on my knees, but I know there was a presence surrounding me that I'd never felt before. When I finally stood up, I knew that everything would be okay. A deposit of faith—a gift from God—permeated my being that day.

Both houses were still listed for sale. We were grateful that Ian's parents held the mortgage on our one house and were not demanding monthly payments. This saved us from losing our deposit on the new build.

The very night that I called out to God, a couple scheduled an appointment to view one of the houses. They put in an offer to rent, and we accepted it. They were from out of town and asked if they could come by the next evening to inquire about schools for their children. They were pastors who were settling in our area and starting a church.

I hadn't told Ian about what had happened to me that morning. We were not engaged in a spiritual life, and I didn't want him thinking I'd gone off the deep end. We were both in rough shape.

Within minutes of the couple's arrival, I began interrogating Pastor Henry about how God could allow such hardship to happen to us—such hard workers. He pulled out his Bible and answered every question—straight from the Word. I understood everything he said. That evening he prayed with me, and I received Jesus into my heart. An animated character, Pastor Grace, told me how God had let her know that I would get saved that night.

Ian thought we were all nuts! He sat there with his arms folded. Two months later, Ian received Christ.

The challenge we came through was minor compared to what we would encounter with Paul. The temporary financial storm taught me about my *Shelter* during the storms of life—my Saviour and Lord, Jesus Christ. I was very hungry for His Word and matured quickly.

A few years after my God encounter, I attended Bible College. Post-graduation, I was offered a pastoral position at a church founded by the pastors who rented one of our houses. In my wildest dreams I never thought I was pastor material, but I knew that I had an intense affection for humanity. I assumed all people felt the same.

Paul taught me that people should not be defined by their behaviour or IQ. I became aware that inappropriate behaviour is usually the side effect of intense pain.

Paul loved going to church. He was well treated, loved, and grew in the Lord. Pastor Grace made church attendance fun. There were times that 75 children attended her class, and Grace kept them all entertained while teaching them rich biblical truths.

When Paul became a teenager, socialization became excruciatingly painful. He was teased, bullied, and humiliated. He was unsuccessful in learning, even in special-ed settings. His self-esteem was constantly eroding, and he was required to change schools several times.

If space allowed, I could tell you hundreds of stories, but this one was, for us, the most traumatic.

I was now engaged in a full-time pastoral position at the church. Paul was about 15 and still small in stature. While visiting one of the parishioners, she told me about a doctor who was known for successfully helping people with disabilities like Paul's. Our family doctor provided a referral for Paul to see the specialist. Ian and I attended the hour-long assessment with Paul. The doctor asked Paul questions and gave him a surface check. After the examination, the doctor appeared entranced in thought as he sat on the edge of his desk hovering over Paul. He looked at us and said,

"If I were you and this was my son, and I lived in Russia, I would be ordering a lobotomy for him. You need to report his condition to the police so that when he does the violent things he will do, you will not be held responsible." He then dismissed us.

We left the meeting in shock. While driving home Ian began to sob. We were five years into our walk with God and had learned enough to know that this doctor had cursed our son. As we came through the trauma, we applied spiritual wisdom to deal with our experience and sought guidance from God and caring friends. I tried to obtain a written report from the doctor, and he refused. It's possible he sent it to our family doctor, who may have been trying to protect us by not forwarding us a copy.

Our older son received a full scholarship to attend a prestigious music college in Boston. He was the first international, first-year student to receive the Boston Jazz Society Award. He has not lived in Canada since that time. We are so proud of all he accomplished.

Paul was 16 at the time, and his life was miserable. He grew to become 6' 3" with a muscular physique.

Finishing basic-level high school, Paul was deemed a person with a disability by the Province of Ontario. He became a cast member with 'Famous People Players'—a black light theatre troupe featuring people with intellectual disabilities. Paul enjoyed two years with the acting company and grew in his understanding of basic life skills. Paul experienced an injury, and along with the high stress of the job, it caused his inability to continue working for the theatre troupe.

Adult life for Paul continued to be extremely challenging. He easily obtained employment, but it was often short lived due to inappropriate behaviour, which was unbeknownst to him.

Or he would work to the point of exhaustion, sleep into the next day, and not show up for work. Paul repeatedly experienced failure, and disappointment. As his frustration escalated his reactionary behaviour led to assault charges.

When Paul was in his late 20's we were advised by a local police officer to, *"Get him out of town, or he will end up in jail, and 'they'll' kill him."*

Paul had demonstrated an ability to live independently. With Paul's consent, we decided to get him a place in the village where Ian and I had grown up; we had a cottage on the shores of the lake on which the small town was situated.

He had acquired his driver's licence, and we got him a vehicle so he could get around.

During the next 15 years, Paul lived in various houses in the village, including our cottage and a 35-foot house trailer. I often travelled the three-hour trek north to help him come through several surprising situations.

During those years, Almaguin Community Living assisted us in getting Paul an appointment with a psychologist in North Bay to reassess his condition and learn how we could support him. This doctor specialized in people with learning disabilities. The appointment was scheduled for 10 a.m.; we were an hour away from the office. I was at the cottage, Paul was at his place, and Ian was in Oakville working. Arriving at Paul's house I found him sound asleep. When I managed to awaken him, he was furious and raging. I called Ian, asking him to pray for my protection. I persuaded Paul to get in the car, and for the entire trip, he screamed continuously—his head out the window, chain-smoking.

Paul received a dual diagnosis: Mentally Challenged/Mentally ill (Autism Spectrum Disorder, Obsessive Compulsive Disorder & Depression), along with many sub-conditions including lack of impulse control. Each diagnosis of autism spectrum disorder is complicated and unique. This diagnosis helped us support Paul with consideration and respect.

Ian and I found our God-given gifts and talents through these challenging times. We sought God's help through biblical studies and grew in understanding beyond imagination. Neither of us had formal education. Ian retired from the Fire Department at age 51. He developed and ran the Fire & Emergency Program at Humber College in Toronto, retiring at age 70.

I resigned from my position as pastor and founded a charity in 1991–Northern Praise Ministries Inc. Although extremely busy, it afforded me flexible work hours so I could support Paul when needed.

God equipped me to develop an extensive skill set despite my lack of education. I am often reminded of His favour in my life.

Here are some highlights:

- In the early 90s, I coordinated *Canadian Performance and Music Industry* Seminars. Several of the attendees are today, some of my closest friends.

- For years, I hosted monthly meetings for artists, primarily musicians. These sessions provided opportunities for showcasing, recruiting, educating, encouraging and fellowshipping.

- I have produced several events: concerts, women's conferences, and retreats.

- I have provided artists with many opportunities for paid gigs.

- I showcased six Canadian acts at the *U.S. Gospel Music Association's* annual conference in Nashville — a first for a non-record label.

- I have provided many platforms to connect and network artists with other artists and organizations.

- I received a Juno Award, in 2000, for being the Executive Producer of a Best Gospel Album 1999.

- I wrote, produced and directed two plays performed at 'The Oakville Centre for the Performing Arts'—hiring and paying the entire crew and raising substantial funds for The Salvation Army.

- I produced and presented the first-ever Gospel Showcase at Canadian Music Week.
- I brought to Canada a renowned 'On-stage' producer who helped several artists advance in their music careers.
- I am a songwriter, recording artist and vocalist for four CD projects.
- I authored and self-published three books.
- I am a keynote speaker and humorist.
- I am the creator of the "Love Bomb."
- Too many more to mention.

I am not bragging about *my* accomplishments. I am bragging on the **Lord**!

I have applied what I learned, to help others on their journey. All of this was faith-building and rewarding work. Even today, I am in awe of all God has equipped and empowered me to accomplish with excellence.

When given a new challenge, I would say, *"God, I don't know how to do that."*

He replied, *"Well, you're smart. Figure it out!"*

And I would. This insight helped when others approached me and said, *"God asked them to do something, but it was too hard*. I confidently responded, *"If God told you to do it, He knows you can! No excuses!"*

The most grievous heartache was watching all that plagued Paul amidst our successes. While living up north, he began living like a hermit. He was non-compliant with potential supporters. He had lost most of his teeth, and his hygiene was grim.

In the summer of 2015, I felt led by God to study and enter a three-week fast and prayer time. I started on October 1, 2015, at 7:30 a.m. That morning, Paul arrived at our home, having driven three hours from his house trailer. Upon arriving, Paul announced, *"Your prodigal son has come home. Can you prepare me a feast for dinner tonight?"*

Oh, my darling, Paulie! He's been with us ever since.

On the same day, Ian and I attended a wedding where I met a couple who had been praying for a charitable organization. I offered them my charity, having run it successfully for 25 years.

I attended the afternoon wedding and prepared a festive dinner for my son that day! Again, with God's help, I managed. And that, my friends, was just day one of the fast!

At the end of the three-week fast, I had two consecutive speaking engagements in Eastern Ontario. I was operating at a heightened level of confidence and anointing. A new season in my life had begun. The *storm* – our beloved Paul - is still present and living with us full-time.

When I turned 70 in 2018, I thought about retirement. I asked Ian for feedback about a course I was considering taking.

"Do I sign up for the, ***Advance Your Reach*** *course? Or do I hang up my hat?"*

Without hesitation, Ian encouraged me to take the course and keep going.

The course, offered via Zoom, originated in Colorado. I felt my age presented a slight barrier and required cognitive processing to translate the data being presented into manageable information. Several course participants were looking to maximize their annual 'stages.' My goal was five to seven 'stages' a year–anywhere in the world.

Although comfortable in the Zoom meetings, I took a course to enhance my skill set. I also enrolled in a course on running a Mastermind program so I could help as many people as possible without unnecessary travel or expenses. I was constantly brainstorming ways to help people. Thoughts continued, and the idea of creating something called "Love Bombs" came into being.

When I wrote my second book, ***My Son, My Gift...Living with Autistic Spectrum Disorder***, God clearly showed me that the best thing we could do for our struggling son was to love him without conditions. As I reflected, I came across two books written in 1928. The books, ***This Kind of Love*** and ***Christ the Healer***, became the bedrock for creating the Love Bombs. I reasoned that Jesus was always successful in every endeavour He took on because, *He was ALWAYS* motivated by the Love of God, and *ALWAYS* empowered by the Grace of God. Furthermore, Jesus only did and said what His Father asked Him to do and speak.

This became my goal. I was claiming Paul's promised healing. God asked me to write the Love Bombs to reveal His Glory to those watching our journey, believing it will happen.

"But He was wounded for our transgressions, He was bruised for our iniquities; The chastisement for our peace was upon Him, And by His stripes we are healed." Isaiah 53:5 (NKJV)

"...who Himself bore our sins in His own body on the tree, that we, having died to sins, might live for righteousness—by whose stripes you were healed." 1 Peter 2:24 (NKJV)

I began studying and teaching the Book of Acts to my Zoom classes. There is no reason we can't walk as the first century Church walked. Something's been lost over the centuries, and I want it back. My son needs it back. Our world is screaming for deliverance from mental illness, incurable diseases and everything else mentioned in Deuteronomy, Chapter 28. Christ's Blood paid to eradicate it all.

Without a doubt, these last seven years have been the most difficult as our storm has continued to rage. These last two years of wading through COVID restrictions have supplied opportunities to love without conditions on a whole new level. I will not go into details to protect Paul's dignity.

I have noticed that as I write and practice the lessons presented in the Love Bombs, Paul's good days are longer, and his *stormy* days are less. Choosing to react to the difficult days by, 'loving as Jesus loves' has made a significant difference in our family. Paul's healing has been incremental, but it is coming, and God will get all the glory. My 'storm' has become my greatest 'blessing.'

I pray my journey—thus far—will encourage you to keep going.

"Anything worth having is worth fighting for."

Remember, you are not fighting alone. You are fighting with God and His empowering Grace. God loves you.

I know you can do it Love Pastor Michelle

www.MichelleSim.com

Chapter Eight

The Final Answer to Every Question

Beth Fisher

AS AN INHERENT “OVERACHIEVER,” I dreamed of a big life from a very early age.

Having grown up in the Midwest—Northeast Ohio to be exact—I was always in search of more.

Of course, as a precocious five-year-old, no one told me what “*more*“ meant. More than what, I often wondered as I continued to lead with questions? *But why is that okay?*” I asked my parents and teachers.

"But why are those the 'rules'?" I asked my priest? *But who decided that and how was it decided upon?"* I asked everyone in my wake.

To answer my incessant question of (More what?) I first had to understand who, was behind how the world worked, and why the world worked as it did.

That understanding was not easy to come by in my formative years. While I am unwaveringly sentimental about my Midwest roots, I grew up in an impoverished village. In 2020, the United States Census Bureau estimated its population to be 3,482; it was far less when I arrived there with my parents in 1977. From a pure resource perspective, there wasn't many people to ask my ongoing existential questions. From a pure tolerance perspective, I exhausted people.

Today, with the gift of age and retrospect, I get it. I can't tell you how many times I have exhausted myself. Incessant thoughts; questions devoid of logical answers; nonsensical life situations and circumstances. But why is any of this okay? When our brains cannot reconcile disparities, injustices, inequalities, and certainly the unknown—we become tired.

'I know a little something about tired.'

After graduating high school, among a small number of classmates, I went to the largest college in our state: Ohio State University. Free at last! No one knows me! Look how many people there are to interrogate (66,000+ students)! I was only two hours and forty-five minutes south of my hometown, yet I felt like Christopher Columbus exploring a vast new territory with endless possibilities. I was seventeen and away from home for the first time, ready to embark upon my newfound freedom.

Homesickness set in quickly, but I pushed past it. I optimistically believed the answers to life's unknown questions awaited the other side of a four-year degree. Day after day, semester after semester (AKA quarters), year after year, I checked off each requisite class en route to the next destination.

I was one step closer to discovering answers to the growing number of questions in my head.

Less than four years after arriving on campus, I donned a cap and gown, ready to walk across a graduation stage surrounded by thousands of strangers. To call them "classmates" would be a misnomer. I didn't know the multitude of undergraduates any more than they knew me. Each of us is on our journey while, at the same time, living a raucous parallel pit-stop, collectively. Now what do I check off, I wondered the second my diploma was in hand?

Marriage was the socially acceptable answer in the early nineties. It was also the familial expectation, whether perceived or real. My parents have been married for over fifty years. Their parents, my grandparents, were married even longer. Only death separated couples in my Irish-Italian family.

Both my sentimentality and understanding of God come from generations of Catholics.

I was married eight months after graduating from college. Seven months later, I was pregnant with my only child, Olivia (Liv). She was born in February 1997. Had she incubated twenty-two days longer, she would have arrived on the second anniversary of my graduation from Ohio State University.

I had just turned twenty-three years old. Of all the constant questions I asked, none of them were about being a wife or mother. I was interested in worldly, extrinsic conditions. Big picture causes and effects.

Why do some people have fresh water and loving families and others do not? Why do some people believe in God and others did not—or at least not the same one? I was in my little world, ill-equipped, yet so in love with this beautiful newborn—I lacked a childrearing skill set.

I couldn't't think, nor could I sleep. Liv had her days and nights mixed up.

"Because you never sat still during pregnancy, it lulled her to sleep," said her paediatrician.

What I heard was, *"It's your fault."*

I cried—and continued to cry nonstop. Something was wrong with me, although I had no idea what.

During one of my crying fits, Liv's dad came home from work and announced,

"We are moving."

He had been offered and accepted a promotion. Olivia was four months old; I had just returned to work and was struggling—unbeknownst to others. Every morning I became paralyzed with fear as I readied Liv to go to her nanny's apartment, two miles down the road. I was full of guilt, shame, and confusion. How can I leave her? All I wanted to do was scoop her up and hold her all day long. Make sure she was loved and safe from the impending danger in the world. A world I once revered, but now was afraid of for reasons that I could neither place nor understand.

"The job is in another state," my husband told me. *"It's seven hours away."*

Instant tears streamed down my face. While I was used to crying uncontrollably out of nowhere, this was different.

"But why? Do we have to?"

"Yes, you'll be fine."

I cried harder.

Six months after Liv was born, amidst post-partum depression, we moved away from the only home I had ever known. Away from family, close friends, and all familiarity. Never one to give up, I began to setup our new home with our limited furnishings. Had my parents not been there to help, I would have been doing that on my own with Liv slung on my hip. Liv's dad was on a golf trip down south with his buddies, so after a seven-hour drive, I was grateful for my parent's help. After one weekend and two excruciatingly long days of unpacking, I was, "home."

It felt anything but. I was tired, angry, scared, and lonely. My zest for life was gone. The only thing that kept me going and able to feel anything at all was Liv. So, when I almost lost her, it was too much to bear.

The following year, my husband moved back to Ohio—without us. His job did not pan out and neither did our marriage. Our entire relationship had been a whirlwind, from our first night together in college, to our engagement, wedding, and becoming parents'. Shifting sand is an understatement; we were underwater, near-drowning.

My innate questions were magnified inside the church. Having been raised Catholic, our family never missed Mass.

There was one small Catholic Church in the Northeast Ohio village where I grew up. In that church, I made my First Communion, engaged in the sacrament of Confirmation, and married Olivia's dad. It was also where I learned that I was going to hell.

Now, let me pause and say, no one *"taught"* me that presumption outright. Rather, having irresolute answers to my endless questions, it was what I concluded. When we do not have concrete answers, we fill in the blanks.

As Brene Brown famously teaches, *"We fill in the blanks with the stories we tell ourselves."*

I told myself that God only loved me if I was good. Catechism (Sunday school) told me that I was bad. We are sinners in need of a Saviour. Jesus saved us, and therefore we can never do anything "good enough" to repay God. Along with being created as a consummate question-asker, I am also very literal. Cause and effect. Winning and losing. Good and bad. *'I was bad, so I was going to hell.'*

When I was fifteen, I stood next to my boyfriend's mom at the front of our church; ironically, she was my Confirmation sponsor. I'm confident she was aware of my intention to marry her son (as every starry-eyed naive girl intends upon meeting her first crush). I also assumed that she (and our priest) knew we were having premarital sex. In my literal mind, if we were going to get married, premarital was fine.

Inevitable, even. Besides, I confessed and made penance every Sunday before Mass. I said ten Hail Mary prayers that were given to me as punishment, hoping to amend my sin. Except apparently, it did not, and I paid for it for the next thirty years.

As a side note, I found it ironic that the sacrament of Confirmation is called such, as it is meant to mean that the faith given in Baptism is now confirmed and made strong. Sometimes those who go through the sacrament of Confirmation are referred to as "soldiers of Christ," which isn't a military designation, but a spiritual duty to fight the war between good and evil, light and darkness—a war between humanity and all the powers of hell.

Alluding to the fact that I disappointed God caused feelings of weakness and a belief that I was an unlovable dissenter.

I chose to marry Liv's dad, part and parcel of one singular experience. In my misunderstood view of God, I believed that if I did not marry him, after what presumably happened in college, I would go to hell. So, when he told me our marriage was over, I collapsed.

Picking up the pieces amid a crippling life experience seems insurmountable. How can we reconstruct a broken vessel that's been shattered beyond recognition? For me, the answer to reconstructing my life was Liv.

Embracing the reality of my divorce, I confronted my embarrassment, shame, and overwhelming fear of God. I went to work—both literally and figuratively. Now a single parent, I had to devise a plan to create financial sustainability.

The family, "*home*" was sold, and we moved across town to an affordable rental unit. I attempted to earn a living selling business process automation software to companies in a defined territory. There was only one problem: I lacked product knowledge and felt inadequate in my skillset. I was twenty-four, with minimal employment experience.

'Did prior casual employment stints count? Is there an age criterion for engaging in business opportunities? How do I navigate the corporate world?'

I had questions . . . and no one to call on. So, I asked Liv. "*What kind of business products do you think Mommy should sell? Do you think that business needs software? What should we eat for dinner? Would you like to sing that Winnie-the-Pooh song again? Are you okay, my sweet baby girl?*"

Two months passed. Our new rental unit was beginning to feel familiar, as was the town. I was able to navigate my way around town and I memorized the route to Liv's daycare. I worked from a makeshift home office, calling prospects and emailing clients using Lotus Notes and a loud dial-up internet connection. As had been true to date, I learned on the fly. I continued to ask questions—I sought wisdom to navigate life amidst a divorce and guidance in raising my first child while distanced from family.

One day, my office phone rang less than ten minutes after I returned from dropping Liv off at daycare. Excited it might be a customer, I answered on the first ring. *"Hello, this is Beth!"* I said cheerfully.

The caller quietly responded, *"Beth, it's Laura."*

I paused to recall an acquaintance or familiar customer, named Laura. The caller understood my pause indicated confusion, "Your old neighbour." she said, *"Oh, hi! Nice to hear from you!"*

Laura was a neighbour from our old neighbourhood. We resided in a quiet subdivision inhabited by intact families. The houses were complete with grassy yards and welcoming porches. Laura was a wife, a mom, and my doctor.

I had been fighting a nasty cold, the kind that renders you a leper while in the grocery store—a single mom, your hoarse voice interrupted by your sneezing and the stares of others. I stubbornly relented, and finally visited Laura at her office to see about getting an antibiotic.

"I need you to come back to my office," she said.

My stomach dropped. I knew if I had a sinus infection, she wouldn't need to see me again. I knew intrinsically that something was wrong—very wrong—and that something was about to be confirmed.

Before the phone call, it had been easy to blame my inner nagging on the divorce. Nothing feels right during that kind of grief, loss, and impending uncertainty.

"No, I can't," I responded. *"I just started working and I am super busy. Please just tell me whatever you* need to over the phone."

Silence.

In the span of seconds, feeling more like days, Laura asked if I were sure.

As a salesperson, I could sell her on the fact that I was ready to hear whatever it was that she was about to say. But the truth is, I wasn't ready for any of it.

"Your white blood cells are ten times higher than normal counts," she began.

I immediately felt better since, in my mind, that was an easy fix! It was a simple math problem!

"Oh, okay," I said. "*How do we get them back down to normal?"*

"Are you sure you don't want to come to my office so we can talk through this?" she asked.

"Please just tell me," I said. *"There are three possibilities, two of them are cancer. I'm 95% certain you have leukiemia."*

Everything she said after that was a blur. Her words were muffled as if I was submerged underwater. I had no idea what to do, think, or say. I went numb. Hanging up the phone, I sank to the floor.

Curling up in the fetal position, weeping and shaking uncontrollably, my thoughts went to Liv. I pictured her sweet, happy, giggly face. I pictured her tiny snow boots lined up outside of her daycare room; her winter coat hanging on the peg above. When I envisioned her coming home to an empty house, I lost it.

She can't grow up without me, I thought. How will she know how much I loved her?

I slowly composed myself. Leaning against my office desk for support, I raised myself to my knees, then propped my elbows on top of my chair for additional support. Feeling steady, I made the final ascend upright, only to fall again. My legs gave out. My heart hurt: my soul was crushed.

My baby girl...alone. It was more than I could bear. That moment was, by far, the worst part of the storm.

The unknown is always the worst.

After two weeks of waiting, a final diagnosis arrived: leukaemia. A bone marrow biopsy, one of many to come, confirmed the type. I had "Chronic Myeloid Leukaemia" and there was no cure. I was twenty-five years old, in the middle of a divorce with a new baby, a new job, and away from my support system.

The morning Laura called me with the devastating news proved to be, years later, the defining moment of my life. While I didn't know it at that moment—in the eye of the storm—I know it now.

After hanging up the phone and composing myself, I called my dad. Understandably, he was crushed but assured me he would tell my mom and sister, and they would come out to stay with Liv and me until we figured out what to do. Then I went to see my other Dad—God.

Behind the steering wheel, eyes filled with tears, I instinctively drove to the local Catholic Church. I'd never been there and knew no one—but I knew God. It took every ounce of strength I had to drive there. I was still deathly afraid of God.

What kind of oxymoron is that? I'm "dying," and I am "deathly" afraid of God. The God who made me and the God that, assumedly, I'd never get to see since I believed I was going to hell.

I had questions. But for the first time in my life, I didn't ask them.

Perhaps a part of me wasn't simply afraid of God but of myself. Of what I had become; what my life had become. In hindsight, I was tempering my questions under the guise of avoiding the two most quintessential inquiries each of us should ask during our journey: '*Who is God? Who am I?*'

As I sat at the back of the church, there was an immediate sense of peace that washed over me. Was it the familiarity of a Catholic Church, or was it something else? Something else that I didn't deserve since, as a divorced sinner, the only thing I deserved was cancer—which I assumed God gave me, along with a ticket straight to hell when I inevitably died from it. That was my "theological understanding" of God at age twenty-five—cumulative experiences learned from my upbringing, worldview, and experience with earthly relationships.

Man was I wrong.

After thirty-five days of undergoing a Bone Marrow Transplant in my home state of Ohio, I was the only person who walked out alive!

Having befriended others who were in the hospital undergoing transplants for their respective cancers, I watched all of them die, one by one, in five weeks. Nothing made sense. What did they do wrong, I wondered? What kind of sinners were they? While I was incredibly grateful to be alive and going home to Olivia, I didn't understand how that was possible. Did God make a mistake? I thought he gave me cancer as punishment for my divorce. Did He change his mind?

One fellow transplant recipient and friend, Jeff, married his lifelong sweetheart in the hospital. He donned a Grand Poo-bah hat to hide his bald head as he smiled brightly, staring into his bride's eyes. Attached to my chemo pole, I stood behind the nurses' station, watching, crying, and cheering, as they became husband and wife.

Jeff died two days later.

I'll never forget our conversation a week before his passing. Wheeling into his room, he greeted me with his standard, *"Howdy, Partner! It's good to see you!"*

Jeff's smile could light up an airport runway, let alone a sterile hospital room.

"Hey, it's good to see you, too!" I said as I padded over to the visitor chair in his room.

Unlike most of our conversations, the pleasantries stopped quickly that day. Jeff said he had something important to discuss with me.

"Where do you think we go when we die?" he asked.

"Are you serious right now?" I asked him, still deathly afraid of God and hell.

"Yeah, do you believe in God or not?"

I told him the truth. I did, but I was pretty sure God didn't love me after all I had done. I even shared that I believed the reason I had leukaemia was God's punishment for my sins.

"This is why I love you, Beth. You have a heart for God, for others, and the truth. And the truth is, God, loves you and me—and everyone! —so much that he sent Jesus to the cross so all the trouble we get into here on earth is forgiven."

That was my rainbow. I had been trying to find it but was avoiding its sighting. It made more sense to believe I deserved a storm from God than His vibrant forgiveness. I was blind...but now I see.

Unconditional love. It's what got me through then, and it's what gets me through now. God first sent me (and you) Jesus and then He sent me Olivia. From the moment I looked into her eyes, that girl has been my reason for living. I held her close to my chest and whispered, *"I love you baby girl . . . no matter what."*

I have understood what it means to fully love another human, despite their faults and flaws, their offences and wrongdoings. There has never been, nor ever will be, anything Liv can do that will cause me to love her any less.

That experiential understanding, more than any question asked or book read, is what provided me with the awe moment—the rainbow—in my life's storm. I finally understood that the same is true of God.

In God's great mercy, we are forgiven. We are loved and there's nothing we have done or will ever do to change that.

Today, as I embark upon my fiftieth birthday, I am profoundly grateful for all I have been through. My mind, heart, and soul have been transformed throughout my journey—thanks be to God!

Love, Beth

Chapter Nine

Strength, Determination, Focus and Faith

Penny MacCormack

Strength, Determination, Focus and Faith

"We Don't Heal in Isolation—We Heal in Community." ~ S. Kelley Harrell

"Many people have told me that I am an inspiration. It was not my intention to inspire others through my battle with cancer, but rather to support and love others."

My name is Penny MacCormack. On August 2019, at age 48, I was diagnosed with metastatic colon cancer. It is essential that I maintain chemo treatments bi-weekly for the rest of my life—unless alternative treatment options present.

Pre-cancer, I was in optimal shape and conquered life head on. Being diagnosed with cancer is challenging. Upon receiving the diagnosis, my thoughts automatically shifted to family and friends.

'*Would they be okay without me?*'

I decided to use my God given strengths to help me through this battle with cancer. My family, and friends continue to stand with me in this battle.

People have been placed in my life to help me navigate the ebb and flow of my journey. People have offered support by means of attentive listening, words of encouragement, normalizing perspectives, and shared experiences. Situational encounters have both impacted and enhanced my life.

"The greatest rewards come when you give of yourself. It's about bettering the lives of others, being part of something bigger than yourself, and making a positive difference." ~ Nick Vujicic

I have endured 74 chemo sessions to date. After healing from surgery and coming to terms with chemotherapy, I decided to utilize my strength and passion to complete a personal triathlon. The triathlon consisted of kayaking, cycling, and walking a total of twenty-five kilometers. I coordinated the triathlon to raise money for the Juravinski Cancer Centre Chemo Unit—a second home for myself since the onset of my diagnosis. My 50th birthday was on the horizon (May 2021), and I wanted to engage in a memorable experience. The triathlon presented an opportunity to fundraise, help others and redirect my focus—gratitude in action.

I am a firm believer in the importance of community. Community congregates in times of sorrow and joy. It offers support, guidance, encouragement, and confidence.

Community is there when you least expect it. When I was diagnosed with cancer, I was surrounded by many communities: church, work, family, friends and neighbours. In my experience, there are commonalities within social groups, specifically love of people and familiar bonds.

Personally, I have known many people battling cancer, two of which were my parents. My mom battled melanoma cancer for 17 years and my dad multiple myeloma for 9 years. My parents passed, in 2014 and 2015 respectively, so this triathlon was a way for me to commemorate my parents.

Encouragement and prayer offered me a sense of love and belonging. I felt like I was impacting others in a positive way. I was able to view life through a different lens. In a world inundated with negativity, it was refreshing to experience an abundance of love and support.

"Just don't give up trying to do what you really want to do. Where there is love and inspiration, I don't think you can go wrong.' ~ Ella Fitzgerald

In preparation for the triathlon, I began calling on my community supports. Some of my family was concerned for my physical health participating in a triathlon while on chemo. I sought medical support from my oncologist and nursing staff. I gleaned encouragement from friends, and coworkers. Extended communities provided monetary and fundraising support. My initial fundraising goal was $800, which I thought was hefty, but I ended up raising over $20,000.

Massaging my spiritual growth, I prayed for holistic strength, focus and positivity throughout this adventure.

"There are no limits. There are only plateaus, and you must not stay there, you must go beyond them." ~ Bruce Lee

There were people who questioned my participation in the triathlon because I was receiving bi-weekly chemo treatments. Intuitively, I knew they were concerned for my well-being. Those known to me are aware that when I am focused on achieving a goal, I complete it to the best of my ability. People challenged me to, '*Come out of my comfort zone—to put myself out there and advocate for my cause.*'

I thrived in wisdom and understanding and was awakened to the goodness in others. Numerous acts of kindness and generosity did not go unnoticed. My fitness instructor and a friend joined me in fitness training. My daughter created a Facebook page to promote the fundraiser, and Juravinski Fundraising Committee set up a webpage for donations. My son took promotional pictures, a local design company donated t-shirts and monetary donations came in from all walks of life.

People are put in our lives to challenge, support, guide and encourage us. During this time, I learned that our struggles bring out the best in people.

"Nothing is impossible. The word itself says, 'I'M POSSIBLE!'" ~ Audrey Hepburn

I am blessed with an optimistic perspective and a firm belief that nothing is impossible—challenging perhaps—but not impossible. When given an opportunity, you embrace it.

During my good weeks, strength and endurance training were on my agenda. On my chemo weeks, I would strength train pre-chemo and rest five days post chemo.

"Sometimes we need someone to simply be there. Not to fix anything, or to do anything, but just to let us feel that we are cared for and supported."

TRIATHLON DAY:

Two days after my 50th birthday the triathlon was upon us. The event was scheduled a few days before my 43rd round of chemo.

God was smiling down on us that morning. The sun illuminated the calm, peaceful ambiance of the lake. Breathing in the fresh air, I took a moment to ponder the depth of my gratitude. It warmed my heart to see familiar faces there to cheer me on.

We entered the water and climbed into our kayaks. As I began to paddle, I embraced natures beauty and felt blessed for great weather and cheerleaders sporadically lining the shore. As we neared the shoreline to begin the second portion of the triathlon, I noticed a small crowd cheering us on with cow bells and pompoms.

We completed the 10 km bike portion in record time. The training paid off; my endurance was steadfast. I am thankful that, despite the cancer, I maintain energy and "good" health.

With the last portion of the triathlon to complete we stopped for photos and reflected on the day's events. Our walking pace was fast as we headed out on the final stretch of the triathlon. Nearing the finish line, we could hear the crowd cheering and ringing cow bells. Feeling overwhelmed with emotions we jogged to the finish line.

I felt elated! I completed the challenge and created opportunities to support other families. ***GOAL*** completed, or is it? Next goal is either jogging the five-kilometre Terry Fox Run with my oncologist or a second annual triathlon—or maybe both. Yes, I said, *"jog. Why not embrace every opportunity given to me?'*

"Difficult roads often lead to beautiful destinations."

~ Author Unknown

Although cancer is something I would not wish upon anyone, I believe my battle with cancer has made me a better person. I am a vocal and engaged advocate for others. I am now a member of the 'Patient and Family Advisory Council' with Hamilton Health Sciences.

Despite my independent nature, I am more willing to ask for help. I have a deeper appreciation of both nature and human interaction. I express gratitude for life's hidden treasures—rhythmic flow of the clouds, interaction of animals, a flowers fragrance, the texture of tree bark, a twinkle in someone's eye.

Moving forward, I hope to help others by personal sharing, offering support, extending a smile, paying it forward, being optimistic and maintaining a sense of humour. On a lighter note, chemo has saved me time and money for things like shampoo, haircuts and shaving my legs! Fortunately, I have people who can laugh with me during the unpleasant experiences of my journey.

"Life isn't meant to be easy; it's meant to be lived. Sometimes good, other times rough. But with every up and down, you learn lessons that make you strong."

Some of the lessons I have embraced throughout my journey with cancer are:

1. Do what you can today because tomorrow is not promised.

2. Inspire others by your actions.

3. Make someone smile, it may be the best part of their day.

4. Laughter, and a wonderful sense of humour are good medicine.

5. Allow people to bless you during life's challenges.

6. Live life to the fullest–there is more to life than thinning hair and lack of eyebrows/eyelashes.

7. Greet each day with gratitude, it's a new day.

8. Open your senses to the beauty that surrounds you.

'You can't have a rainbow without rain and sunshine.'

In life there will be storms, but what matters is how we choose to respond to the storms. I have determined to dance through my cancer storm with grace and perseverance. I have experienced moments of tears and sorrow, but I must move forward. I surround myself with positive people, keep the faith and continue to help others. I maintain a regime of exercise, laugher, and optimism.

A rainbow is made up of many colours, each having different meanings. When pondering the significance of each colour I was able to correlate them to my personal rainbow.

RED represents life, health, vigour, courage, and love. The common thread of these representations is passion. I believe we all demonstrate courage when facing the storms of life. I am determined to use my experience, strength and hope to help others through their cancer journeys. Red represents friends, family, pets and faith, all of whom fill my heart with love, and courage as I endeavour to move forward...

ORANGE represents energy, vitality, cheer, excitement, and adventure. Now, about the energy proclamation! During chemo weeks I have learned to listen to my body. On a good week I enjoy venturing out in nature. Nature provides me with energy, vitality, joy, and excitement. Nature is my happy place; it is scientifically proven to be mood altering! I look at nature with awe and wonder.

YELLOW constitutes happiness, warmth and sunshine. Yellow embraces the beauty of the sunrise, sunset and sun's warming rays. I visualize the colour yellow when I think of people in my life that offer warmth and comfort through acts of love, kindness and compassion. I experience happiness at Juravinski when I am greeted by the smiling concierge, COVID screeners, lab techs, receptionists, oncologist, oncology nurse, chemo nurses, cleaning staff, volunteers etc.

GREEN can evoke powerful emotions, especially when we think of growth, renewal, life, and abundance. Green is associated with feelings of refreshment, peace, rest and security. My journey has evoked powerful emotions.

My intention is not to deny the negative feelings but rather to look at the underlying issues. For instance, feeling sad and frustrated because I long to spend more time with family and friends, but choosing to be grateful for treasured moments together. Sometimes we forget to appreciate life's little blessings.

BLUE has a litany of connotations from sky, sea, expanse and freedom, to intuition, imagination, inspiration, sensitivity, faith and intelligence. I believe my rainbow focus here is inspiration and faith. Every day I am inspired by people, places and situations. We all have challenges to overcome, how we choose to respond is what matters.

Many people have inspired me throughout my cancer journey. My parents handled their cancer journey with determination. Trey Mancini (Baltimore Orioles) fought stage three colon cancer and went on to complete his role in major league baseball.

Nightbirde, singer from ***America's Got Talent***, fought cancer with grace, love and wisdom.

"Not denial, but rebellious hope. Don't you want to see what happens if you don't give up? You can't wait until life isn't hard, before you decide to be happy" ~ Nightbirde

'I continue to be inspired daily by people who demonstrate; resilience, appreciation, gratitude and perseverance.'

INDIGO represents devotion and wisdom. I believe my struggles have presented opportunities to grow in both wisdom and devotion. I have learned that helping others teaches me to replace fear with faith.

Maya Angelou said it best, *"The desire to reach for the stars is ambitious. The desire to reach hearts is wise."*

VIOLET represents ambition. I am blessed with opportunities to be ambitious while reaching the hearts of others. Seventy-four chemo sessions in and determined to push on. My hope is that each of you sees beauty in both rainbows and storms. Our expiry dates are unknown, so until then, walk in faith, exhibit love, and *be a rainbow in someone else's' cloud*.

PS: I have completed my Second Annual Triathlon for a Cure - raising over $7000 for the Juravinski Cancer Centre.

September/18th/2022 my oncologist, his family, myself and my goddaughter teamed up to take part in the Terry Fox Run and with the help of our sponsors we raised over $10000 for cancer research.

'Pushing forward with faith and love.'

Penny

Chapter Ten

COVID, Chicken and a Miracle

Sarah VanNetten

IT IS AN HONOUR to share my story, as contributing author, with such an amazing group of women. I hope each chapter leaves you feeling inspired, blessed, joy-filled and in awe of God's greatness.

As for my story, I never classified myself as an author. I didn't grow up wanting to be a writer. I love to read, but never envisioned myself in the current role of penning aspects of my life destined for publication.

'In hindsight, are any of us where we dreamt, we would be?'

My name is Sarah VanNetten. I am 47 years of age and married to Mike—husband of 21 years. Together we parent four young adults. Zack is 19 years old and attending his first year at Brock University. The twins, Ryan and Alexis, are 17 years old and in grade 12, and Holly is 14 years old and in grade nine.

We live on our family chicken farm in the small-town community of Simcoe. Both Mike and I were raised in the Christian faith and have parented our kids with a love for Jesus and a desire to follow in God's ways. We are the quintessential family, demonstrating strong work ethics, and family values. We love competitive sports and hold our family and friends in high esteem.

Since the storm raged through our lives people have asked, '*Where I envisioned my life was headed?*'

Pre-storm, I thought about a future filled with common desires including health, happiness and embracing family memories with Mike. I looked forward to our annual cottage retreats at Turkey Point—when one retreat ended, the countdown to the following year began. I ruminated, with excitement, about future opportunities for my kids. I wasn't one to entertain wild, crazy dreams. I found joy in the simple things in life and was known for my frugal nature—I can stretch a penny a long way!

Throughout the pandemic, the lockdowns presented opportunities to learn how to grow in contentment and happiness. I missed the busyness of life, yet I enjoyed cooking and family mealtime. I loved spending time with Mike and the kids—my chosen companions during mandatory lockdowns! Like most, I hoped the world would right itself. In the interim, I chose to carry on and make the most of the situation.

It became blazingly obvious to me that each new day presents uncertainty. We often take for granted how quickly life can change.

'Can you anticipate your whole world being uprooted? Can you envision your life dramatically changing with the simple act of opening your eyes in the morning? Can you imagine the turbulence of a storm that shakes you to the core of your being?'

In April 2021, society had been navigating through the uncertainty of a global pandemic for over a year. It changed the way we lived; it changed life as we knew it. At the onset of the pandemic, many people we knew were unaffected and observed from a distance.

On April 8th, I became directly affected when my husband took ill and was diagnosed with Covid-19. We had done our best to abide by public health guidelines, but we still worked the farm and had outside jobs to attend. Despite our best efforts, it wasn't enough to defy the virus. I struggle to refer to Covid as a virus—admittedly the word sounds trite. From my perspective, it is a disease that presents no rhyme or reason who it attacks—it's a monster!

Throughout the days leading up to April 8th Mike had not felt well. I assumed it was the flu—the '*man*' flu. Looking back, I have trouble forgiving myself for feeling irritated with his lack of energy.

'Why did I waste my energy entertaining anger?'

He was not eating or sleeping well. I began to feel a nag on my heart and conscience. Mike wasn't improving—by now he should have been exhibiting signs of improvement! Fear and uncertainty began to grip me.

On, April 8th Mike's breathing was laboured. He was, for lack of better words, beside himself. When I asked, *if he wanted to go to the hospital?*

He answered, "*Yes.*"

It was likely, one of the scariest *yes's* I have ever heard.

I immediately drove him to the hospital. Arriving at Norfolk General Hospital, I drove to the emergency entrance. Unable to go in with him due to Covid restrictions, I extended love and watched him walk through the doors alone. Unbeknownst to me, 35 long days would pass before my eyes would embrace his again. It was in that moment that I entered the worst storm of my life.

"*In this world you will have trouble. But take heart! I have overcome the world.*" (John 16:33)

'*As I ponder the succession of events, it still feels so fresh—so raw. I can vividly recall the paralyzing fear. I can recap the taunting emotional roller coaster—the numbness and fear of the unknown.*'

Observing Mike walk through the doors of the Norfolk General Hospital was just the beginning. Within an hour of his arrival Mike was diagnosed with Covid-19—a case too far advanced for our small-town hospital. He was taken by ambulance to Joseph Brant Hospital in Burlington. Mike suspected he would be in hospital for three days. Although I remember every detail of the events following his admission, Mike's memory was hazy.

'*How would I cope without him—even for three days? What would I tell our kids? What would I tell our family and friends? How would I manage the farm without him? How would I navigate this storm when the person who always ensured me everything would be ok, couldn't be that person for me right now?*'

I have always loved God and actively maintain a life of prayer and gratitude. I have witnessed God in sunrises, in smiles and in the beauty of a lightning storm over the lake. I actively engaged God in conversation during the year preceding our storm.

In July 2020 we lost Mike's mom, Tina, to cancer. I saw God at work during her final days. Her love for the Lord never wavered, and one's faith could only be strengthened by observing the way she fought her battle.

During the tumultuous days of our storm, I held fast to the words of Tina's favourite song, *10,000 Reasons.*

"And on that day when my strength is failing, the end draws near, and my time has come. Still my soul will sing your praise unending, ten thousand years, and then forever more".

I grew up regularly attending Sunday school. Admittedly, I am not well versed in bible stories nor quoting scripture, but I do know the power of God's word. I know who God is, I knew I needed him, and I knew this storm was too big for me. Storms allow trees to take deeper roots and the roots of my faith needed to deepen.

I started my '*journaling*' journey on the first night of Mike's hospital stay. Facebook was the platform I used for journal entries. My first post reflected the depth of my shock, fear and anger. I wanted to tell people of Mike's situation and warn others that the virus was no respecter of persons. I asked for prayer. I encouraged those who doubted to realize that Covid was real!

Looking back, I realize that my first post ended with, "Be still and let God. He is our only hope." That first day, despite the depth of my fear, I knew we needed God—our *Shield*.

I felt I was living a nightmare. The storm worsened. On April 10th, I received a call from staff at the Burlington Hospital. They advised me that Mike's best chance of recovery was to be placed on a ventilator. My worst fear was becoming a reality. I spoke with Mike on the phone before they vented him and ultimately induced a medical coma. I couldn't begin to imagine his fear.

'How do I summarize the depth of my love for Mike in only a few moments? How do I show him how much he means to me? How do I tell him to fight and never give up?'

God is not a God of coincidences. Mike's grade school friend was also at Joe Brant Hospital, diagnosed with Covid and placed on a ventilator. Mike's friend came off the ventilator just as doctors determined Mike's need. I believe that God orchestrated the timely availability for a ventilator for Mike—a machine that could save Mike's life too.

Currently, Mike's friend is also a Covid survivor and doing well!

After my phone call with Mike, I remember fear washing over me. In the moments that followed, I messaged family and friends asking them to flood Mike's phone with positive, uplifting words of encouragement. I wanted Mike to feel overwhelmed with love before they vented him. I soon learned how long a day can feel. I learned that, despite numbness, hours continue to pass. I intuitively knew that I needed to continue giving my fears to God.

"Have I not commanded you? Be strong and courageous. Do not be afraid; do not be discouraged, for the Lord your God will be with you wherever you go." (Joshua 1:9)

On April 13th, I thought I couldn't possibly feel more afraid—I found out I was wrong. I was advised, by staff at Joe Brant Hospital, that Mike was a match for a procedure that would place him on an Extracorporeal Membrane Oxygenation (ECMO) machine—AKA life support machine. The machine would replace the function of his lungs. It was his best chance for survival.

This machine was traditionally used by people awaiting lung transplants but was now used by Covid patients. It would pump blood from his body to an artificial lung (oxygenator) that adds oxygen to it and removes carbon dioxide. The ECMO machine then sends the blood back to his body via a pump with the same force as his heart. It gave his lungs a chance to rest.

He would need to be airlifted to Hamilton General Hospital immediately. I did not second guess the doctors. They presented the ECMO machine as an opportunity for healing, but the fear of what was unfolding before me was enormous. I never researched the success of the ECMO machine, I didn't want to. This was Mike's chance to live. I had to believe the doctors knew the best course of action.

On day eight of Mike's hospitalization, I was finally able to see him in person. Prior to my in-person visit, he was blessed with amazing doctors, nurses and social workers. They were available to talk to me whenever I requested an update. They arranged Facetime videos to avoid the shock of seeing Mike hooked up to all the tubes and machines. I can't even imagine the impact on the workers as they connect with a patient's loved one to answer questions and witness their tears and pain through a video screen. It was overwhelming to believe that only eight days ago I drove Mike to the emergency department, and now he lay so still and quiet in the Intensive Care Unit (ICU).

ICU is like no place on earth, a place I hope you never have to experience. I was in awe as I observed the continual bustle in the hallway, the lifesaving conversations, the fragility of information exchanged and the extended efforts to heal and care. The silence seemed to intensify the rhythmic sound of ventilators and machines that were keeping people alive.

'*How did I get here? How have I come to learn medical information that I never deemed relevant in my lifetime?*'

The days seemed long, and the nights seemed endless. When faced with situations in life that are outside of our control, we can choose to focus on things within our control—our response. We can control our response to what is happening in our lives. We can choose our reactions. We can choose how to carry on.

I remember the moment I realized my purpose in life. My purpose, simply, was Mike. My purpose was doing everything within my power to keep him alive—to give him the will to live. I was familiar with setting goals in my life, but never felt I had a purpose.

'Why did I choose not to lay in bed filled with sorrow, refusing to get up? Because if I gave up, how could I expect Mike to fight?'

I chose to have faith in his team of doctors and nurses. I chose to believe for a miracle. I chose to fight for my purpose.

I journaled nightly. I knew that I needed God, and Mike needed prayer. I asked people to prayer for Mike's healing. I prayed for each specific issue he was facing on any given day. I posted journal entries about my prayers for Mike, and I spoke of my love taps. After every visit with Mike, I would tap his wrist, so he knew how much he was loved. I poured my heart into those posts, and as I did, more and more people followed. People prayed, wished, and hoped for Mike's healing. People cried over the setbacks and celebrated the baby steps forward.

Because I had faith does not discredit the fact that I was afraid. I experienced fear unlike anything I had never known, fear that would take my breath away in the quiet of the night. I have never before fallen on my knees screaming and crying out to God. The beautiful irony is that the very things that try to destroy us end up making us stronger.

I have learned that Jesus never promised a life free of pain but rather peace to endure the storms. I felt God with me. I felt his calm surround me. When I felt weak, He strengthened me.

'When you feel like you are drowning, don't worry, your lifeguard walks on water.'

What a comfort.

Mike spent over 30 days in a medically induced coma hooked up to life support equipment. I learned not to get excited with improvements, nor panicked with setbacks.

Mike's healing was a process. We had to keep trying, keep fighting, keep going. I was confidence that the ICU team were doing everything humanly possible to keep Mike alive until I returned the following day.

Sometimes miracles are just good people with kind hearts. I could write a book on the support I received at home. I struggle to find words that adequately express the gratitude I feel for my squad and friends.

I experienced two miracles (rainbows) at the Hamilton General Hospital. The first was a respiratory therapist who was from our hometown. She explained things in a clear, comprehendible manner. She greeted me at ICU when I arrived scared to the bone. She offered hugs when hugging wasn't allowed. She spent countless hours sitting with Mike in his silence. She talked to him while he was awake and recovering. God put this special *angel in scrubs* in our path for a reason.

The second miracle was our cousin who was a nurse on the ICU floor. I called her when I learned that Mike was being flown to Hamilton General Hospital to be put on ECMO.

She said to me, *"Now you are coming to my world."*

What a world it was. She became known for her catch phrase, "*Steady as we go*."

When I wanted to express happiness she replied, *"Steady as we go."*

When I wanted to scream and cry, she replied,

"Steady as we go."

And so, it began, "*Steady as we go,"* became our journey's motto. It grounded me and enabled me to stay steady.

My cousin expressed respect and trust for Mike's doctors. She attended doctors' meetings with me and looked on through Mike's window while procedures were done. She introduced me to the Chaplin because she knew faith was important to me. God puts people in our path to offer shelter in the storms of life.

To be honest sometimes I think I could write novels on what I felt, what I believed, and who I met. Our journey continued through the days—*Steady as we go. Steady as we go,* accomplishing the next right thing. Something good happened, share a tiny smile and refocus. Experience a setback, shed a tear and refocus.

I don't think I could write about this journey without taking a moment to acknowledge the medical professionals—everyone from screeners, cafeteria and cleaning staff to doctors and nurses.

The ICU staff became my pseudo family. Their attentiveness, empathy, kindness, and utter brilliance was second to none. Mike's miracle was, in part, inclusive of the medical team. God is the God of all healing and miracles, but he also equips and positions people to aid in the miraculous.

One of Mike's doctors, a gifted 40-year-old man, said to me, *"Successful people do the optional stuff."*

I replied, *"Thank you for never missing anything optional!"*

'What would life be like if we all adopted a similar mindset? Can you imagine a world where people went the extra mile to help others and maintained a humble, altruistic optimism? Can you imagine communities and family systems that embraced opportunities to learn and grow—as gifts?

What a wonderful world, a world filled with people who uplift others.

The beauty about storms is the ability to recognize the rainbows. Noah didn't stop building the ark to explain himself to every doubter and hater. He kept building and let the rain speak for itself. God's rainbows are a promise of his love for us.

On day eight of our journey a rainbow appeared over our farm. It extended right over the chicken barn--Mike's chicken barn.

"I am with you, always until the end of time." (Matthew 28:20)

Mike was in a coma for over 30 days. He woke up from his coma gradually. It was a slow process that involved trials and errors to ease his anxieties, control systemic levels, and monitor pain.

On day 33 he was taken off the ECMO machine—a ginormous answer to prayer. I remember walking into his room the day after he was taken off the ECMO machine. I observed the ECMO team standing at the foot of Mike's bed, each had giant eye smiles and were chattering about the amazing news—the procedure was a success! I stood in silence, affording them a moment to celebrate a successful step in saving a life.

We still had a long road ahead, a road where the end was often blinded by the curves. The next part of our journey involved rehabilitation, re-building and re-learning. As my wise cousin said, "Now we embrace determination, and *no* is not an option. A brief compromise is the solution, and the goal is going home."

Rehab had its' trials, frustrations and discouragements. Prayer was needed. Mike had to completely relearn the art of sitting, balancing, standing, and walking. He went from a ventilator to a tracheotomy, to relearning to breathe on his own. He relearned how to cough, and how to swallow water.

'*When is it time to try food?*'

Learning to be still and trust God was challenging to say the least. I remember one morning. It was the first morning I had not called the hospital, at 5:30 a.m., for the night nurse's report. Mike was capable of texting now, so I would communicate directly with him. At 7:00 a.m. I asked him, how his night was?

He responded, "*Not good...fever.*"

'*Did we come this far to have a fever set us back?*'

I quickly called his nurse to obtain reassurance. The nurse confirmed he had a fever during the night but assured me that the team figured out the cause.

This was the first time Mike was awake for a setback and he was scared. His fear heightened when he saw how quickly people reacted and surrounded his bed to assess the situation. I arrived that morning to find him resting. I said, "*Mike, I have put every ounce of trust in these people and in God for the past 30 days. I am not going to stop now. Believe in them and believe in God. Sometimes we need to be reminded to breathe—just breathe.*"

Mike had an attitude that was contagious. He set goals. He revealed his personality to his physio team and nurses, a personality that I missed.

A personality filled with laughter and encouragement. His success was their success. Mike's first walk down the hall with his walker was 40 feet round trip and applauded with cheers and tears from onlookers. Many people had been fighting illness for a year and needed a success story as much as me. Sometimes you can't wait for the storm to pass, you need to dance your way through it.

On June 30, with a sendoff to Kenny Rogers, The Gambler, Mike walked out of the Rehabilitation Centre unaided by a mobility device! He was greeted by applause from media, health care workers, and our hospital family...a miracle.

As I sit and reflect, I pen these words with water leaking out of my eyes. I share this journey with Mike by my side. Someone once said, "*God's grace is not the light at the end of the tunnel, it's the light that guides us through.*"

It's true, his grace guided me through the storm. Often the tunnel was riddled with unexpected darkness, corners and bends. God's peace guided me around the twists and turns. I would never wish this storm on anyone, but I welcome opportunities to share about the lessons and rainbows amidst the storm.

I am beyond proud of Mike and of myself. Throughout the storm, I took on the role of advocate and, at times, continue that role today. Mike is the only person I know who was strong enough to endure the battle. He touched so many lives through his recovery. This experience enlarged Mike's circle of friends.

Knowing Mike needed prayer, I asked for it. Thousands of people were storming heaven on Mike's behalf. People prayed for God to raise up *a David,* within Mike, to fight this *Goliath*. People who had no prior relationship with God were suddenly talking to Him. People asked, *"How do I pray?"* There is no right or wrong way to pray. Talk to God like you would talk to a friend. Don't worry about what to ask for, the Holy Spirit knows. God loves to hear from us. I pray that people continue talking to God, prayer warriors continue warring for others and the power of prayer continues to grow.

I was able to experience the beauty of our medical system firsthand and on an extremely personal level. I witnessed staff who continued to show up despite being overworked, tired, and exhausted. I felt led to tell the world (as far as my reach would allow) of the selfless efforts exhibited by the front-line workers. They shed tears of sadness over losses and radiant eye smiles over victories. My heart continues to overflow with love and gratitude. Gratitude is the memory of the heart.

I still feel very strongly about the vaccine. I realize this is a touchy subject, but I am unable to share about experiencing rainbows without mention of the vaccine. I am convinced that if Mike was eligible to receive the vaccine prior to taking ill, our story would not have been so difficult. Several people chose to get the vaccine because of Mike's experience. I felt happy to receive pictures of strangers getting their vaccine.

I struggled to understand those who chose to argue science, especially when I saw medical teams working around the clock to save people. I believe the impact of Mike's journey inspired several people to get vaccinated—another rainbow in the storm.

On one of my nightly posts I quoted, *"Instead of waiting for the storm to pass, dance your way through it. The storm will end, but how will we get through it?"*

I am proud of myself for choosing to share our journey publicly. Behind every scar is the untold story of a survivor. When I look at Mike, I see many scars. I see the little scar on the side of his nose that always seemed to bleed. There is a scar on the side of his neck that held the ECMO needle, one on his chin from the tubing and a mark on his throat from the trach. I can touch them, and I know how blessed I am to have Mike by my side. I see the survivor in both of us.

God wants to show His power through the storms of life. He wants to displace the worries that often linger in the center of our storms. I am confident that through our journey, people experienced the power of God. They saw human weakness, and fear overcome through prayer and petition. They saw God holding us up. He held us as high as we needed to be at any given time in order to survive the storm. It takes time to recuperate from a storm—to begin to recover, to see brighter days.

'How is my life different? It has changed forever and always. How could you come so close to losing the love of your life and not be changed?'

I like to think I changed for the better—I found greater purpose in life. My faith is stronger, and I feel a deeper connection to God in my life.

I was asked, "Was I ever mad at God during this time?" I said, "No, God helped me endure the storm." I was, however, mad at my circumstances. I was mad at Covid. I was mad at people who didn't understand it, nor took it seriously.

Bad things can happen to good people. We were never meant to understand God's ways. We are called to walk in faith, and trust that God will help us live above the circumstances of our storms.

I knew that Mike needed God. Every miracle in the bible was preceded by suffering. I gave Mike's suffering to God daily. I grasped a childlike faith—Let go and let God.

After Mike came home, I couldn't look to the future. I knew that life could change in the blink of an eye. I had witnessed a miracle. I have learned that today is a gift, and the future is not promised. It is in the present moment that we find God.

'How could I possibly have hopes for a future when I had already asked and received so much from God?'

I didn't feel I was entitled. But God wants us to be excited about the life he has given us—the gift of life.

God will see us through this pandemic—this too shall pass. In God's time, not ours. He wants us to look to the future, to make plans, to be excited about events and dreams. God wants us to keep Him at the centre of everything we do in life. When we feel unclear about worldly events, He wants us to seek Him. God wants us to include Him in our decision making. God's gift to us is our life—what we choose to do with it is our gift to God.

I came to realize that experiencing one storm, does not guarantee a storm free future. To be honest, that terrifies me, but I know that nothing is gained from fear or worry.

"Do not fear, for I am with you; I will strengthen you and help you." (Isaiah 41:10)

"Therefore, do not worry about tomorrow, for tomorrow will worry about itself. Each day has enough trouble of its own." (Matthew 6:34)

I am so grateful for the strength and encouragement offered to me by friends. I hope, as they navigate storms in life, I can offer them the strength they so freely gave to me. I hope to bless others through words of encouragement. I hope to be a leader in faith.

This storm has blessed me with the gift of strength and endurance. I have felt the power of prayer and God's peace. I know what it means to grasp rainbows and to come through the storm, a different, stronger version of me—of us.

Steady as we go.

Love Sarah

Chapter Eleven

The Road Home

Jill Cornell

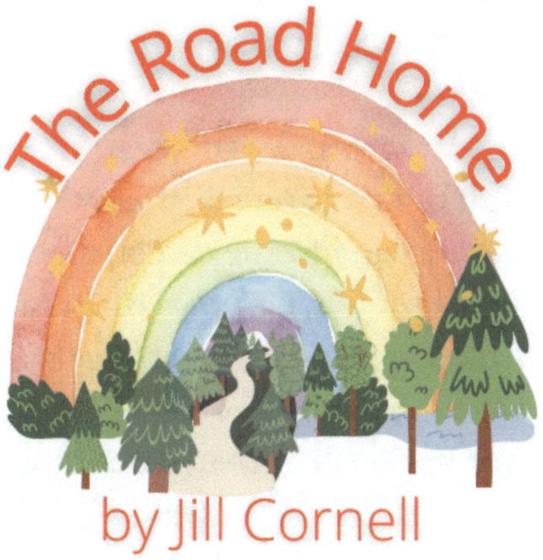

WHEN TRYING TO DEFINE my moment for this book, I felt overwhelmed and lost. I was trying to recapture a past version of myself that no longer existed and struggling to find me. It was in that moment, of loss and reflection, that I was found and saw my rainbow—a bright colourful burst of light that filled my very being.

My rainbow, my promise of a new beginning is a bridge; the answer to prayers, to finding a different way and a new path to become truly me. I didn't realize how desperately I needed this change. I was buried in a sea of conditions, false beliefs, shame and fear. I felt cut off from my inner light and connection to our Creator.

On the evening of August 3, 2021, I wasn't feeling well—completely out of sorts. I was burnt out from the challenges of a demanding job working from home. I had a broken foot, and I was completely worn down by what my post-covid life had become. I was tired and defeated.

I took a hot shower hoping for a chance to regroup and recharge—I thought it would ease my mind and pain. As the water trickled over me, instead of feeling renewed, I felt the opposite. I sensed my life force washing down the drain with the shower water, followed by a complete inability to breath.

I shut off the water and toppled out of the shower, laying in a heap on the floor. I gasped for air that would not come. Everything around me was spinning, I was slowly being swallowed up in darkness. In the distance, I could hear a rainforest waterfall that was not of this world.

I lifted my head, moving in the direction of the comforting sound of trickling water when a voice filled my being and said, *"Not yet Jill. I need you to live; it's not your time."*

I felt an overwhelming wave of peace and calm. The voice was mine, and not mine, all at the same time. Instantly, I was able to gasp for air and call for help. My husband, Kevin, and daughter, Charlotte, rushed to my side. They helped me get up and moved me to the comfort of my bed.

What followed was a heavy analysis of what happened to me. If you know my family you would chuckle at this meeting of the minds; dissecting, overthinking and getting to the source of the matter, is what we do best.

After much discussion and review, I convinced my family and myself that I was okay. I assured them that the *"spell,"* was most likely just a panic attack, resulting from a very stressful and chaotic workload. I told them I just needed to rest and to regroup from my moment of weakness.

Much to my daughter's disapproval, we decided to wait until the morning before seeking any medical care.

Sleep did not come easy that night, as I started to feel nauseous, have chest pain and continued to have rapid breathing attacks. With everything that was going wrong, not once did I change my mind about going to the hospital. I held steadfastly held to the plan to wait and see how I felt in the morning, most certain that my inability to manage anxiety and stress was the cause of what ailed me.

When morning came, I felt stronger and somewhat better. My breath came back, and we all resumed our daily routine. Charlotte and Kevin headed off to work, me to my desk and my son, Jonah, settled in for a typical teenage summer day.

By lunchtime, I knew something was wrong. The gasping for breath returned with the simplest tasks, like going to the washroom. I asked Jonah to call his dad home from work and take me to the hospital. Kevin's drive home is at least 20 minutes. I remember sitting on the couch, rocking, and praying to hang on until he came home. I hid my fears from my son, as I knew something was gravely wrong with me.

Luckily, the local hospital is a few blocks down the street.

Once Kevin came home, we quickly made our way to the ER. I was triaged immediately after explaining how I couldn't breathe. They took my oxygen levels and blood pressure. The nurse calmly took my purse from my hands, gave it to Kevin and told him to take care of registering me. Then, gently guiding me, they explained they had a place for me.

Never, in my lifetime of experiences at our hospital had I seen anyone so quickly processed for care in the ER. I braced myself for what was to come, as I knew it wasn't good. What ensued was a barrage of tests: blood drawn, bedside electrocardiogram, chest x-ray and hooked up to oxygen and monitors. I was fortunate and blessed that our hospital has a state-of-the-art CT scan and that night, there was the absolute perfect mix of healthcare professionals.

By early evening, I was diagnosed with a bilateral saddle pulmonary embolism (PE); my lungs were full of blood clots and my heart was strained. More than once my attending doctor told me that I was lucky to be alive.

I was administered medication to prevent any further blood clots from forming and admitted to the Intensive Care Unit (ICU) for the night.

That evening, the quiet stillness and darkness of the ICU enveloped me in a shadow that I could not escape from or ignore. Loneliness and despair settled in and in no way was I prepared for what was to come.

The immediate days following my diagnoses were a blur. I was released from the hospital after two days, armed with my lifesaving meds and the ability to breath without the need for extra oxygen.

Simple tasks like climbing stairs or bending over to put on my shoes, would leave me breathless and exhausted; a trip to the washroom would be followed by the need to rest. My chest ached in stabbing pain with every waking breath, followed by waves of fear, wondering if I was having a relapse.

Falling asleep, my thoughts carried me to the darkness; I was now familiar with thoughts of if I would wake the next morning. Intuitively, I began the ritual of practicing gratitude to combat the fears and told my family how much I loved them.

I have always considered myself spiritual and grateful, but my near-death experience was beginning to spark a more meaningful, deeper knowing.

My healing occurred at the height of the Covid lock downs in Ontario, so it was easy to stay in hermit mode and keep my growing anxiety and stress to myself. I did not want to worry or cause pain for my loved ones, so I started playing a conscious game of *'hide and seek.'* I would seek and share the positive, physical benchmarks of my healing, while hiding the tidal waves of emotions inside me. So, the better my oxygen levels and stamina became, the more I shoved the overwhelming feelings of shame, guilt, loneliness and hurt, deep down inside me. I convinced myself that once I physically recovered from my PE, everything would fall into place, and I could return to the life that I once knew and longed for.

My recovery journey took a turn for the worse. The physical healing all but stopped, throttled by feelings of anguish and confusion.

How could I not know my body was dying? How did I have so little faith in myself that I mistook the symptoms of my PE, for anxiety, stress and failure?

In the moments that my body was growing weaker and weaker, I was looking outside of myself, convinced I was letting everyone down and had brought this all on myself.

I had lost my inner compass; there was no true north or guiding light inside me.

Ruminating in my pain, I stayed in the shadows, watching my life carry on without me. In my darkest days, thoughts crept in that life would be better without me. I knew I needed help. What I was feeling- the hopelessness- and pain, was just too much for me to manage, and I couldn't see a way out.

I utilized all resources available to me, which was an uphill, complicated battle. I spent hours on the phone advocating to get assistance and then finally connecting virtually for therapy appointments. The post-pandemic world of mental health support is overrun, complicated and constrained; there simply was not, and still is not, enough resources to meet the overwhelming demand.

I was shocked to discover that the grief and despair I was feeling, was not a simple case of my inability to cope with stress and anxiety. I was, in fact, experiencing a deep response to trauma. I had absolutely no concept of what trauma was

… not even an inkling of knowing how to equip myself or to handle this new reality that I found myself in.

I slowly began to process the concept of trauma, the events of my illness and sorting out the complex intertwining feelings from thoughts, and recognizing triggers.

I started meditating, deep breathing and practicing mindfulness. I started feeling stronger, more hopeful and forgiving of my myself. Just when I thought I was on a roll, another curve ball hit me on my healing journey.

I guess I was naïve in thinking that once I identified the trauma and understood the source of my triggers, that the triggers and the post-traumatic stress would simply go away. Right!?

Yet another mistaken belief had been unearthed. The triggers never go away, but I had all the power to manage them in my reactions when I became the observer of my feelings.

I enrolled in an online behavioural, cognitive therapy program. I started practicing mindfulness and actively living in gratitude. All seemed to be going well; I was journaling, reading, resting and rehabilitating when, an astonishing, horrifying and brilliant thing happened. In working through the trauma of my illness, I opened a floodgate of all my past buried traumas and hurts. These long-ignored pains were begging to be acknowledged and released in the name of healing.

The best way to describe what happened to me, was I felt as though I had been hung upside down by the ankles, and shook to my core, until every single hurt fell out of me to be consciously acknowledged. Imagine replaying all the times in your life that you felt unloved, unwanted, too small, too big, ashamed and hopeless reel after reel, blow after blow, sitting there in a front row seat to your lifetime of grief.

As I processed this cathartic moment, I realized that I wasn't feeling my grief and heartache; I was the observer, coming from a place of understanding, love, compassion and connection.

A greater knowing swept over me, one of realization and release. All the stories that I carried and hid deep in my heart and my head, no longer serviced me. These very well-crafted stories I would tell myself no longer made sense. They were in the past—all I have is this moment, right here and now. I realized that I could rewrite all the rules and conditions written by my ego and unconscious self-rules that were created to protect me and keep me safe. I felt a magical, beautiful release and no longer felt my lifetime of self-inflicted burdens.

Upon this release I was transported back in time to watch my eight-year-old self-right right down to my freckles. I was playing on the floor, humming a tune, and dreaming about the person I would become. I knew, in my heart, that I couldn't let her down. She was so full of hope and excitement - she believed she could fly.

Then the most magical thing happened. She looked up at me and smiled, with a loving look of admiration, and spoke these words that forever changed me, *"I can't wait to be you."*

It was in that moment, that I realized a connection to self that went far beyond my physical being and for the first time in a very long time, I felt I belonged.

As I mentioned earlier, I have always considered myself spiritual and felt a deep abiding love of God, but it was complicated and felt external. From the time I was a young adult, I have always looked outside myself for all the answers in life. I looked to others for validation, acceptance and direction. I based my self-worth on how I felt that others perceived me, which is a double edged sword. As wonderful as the accolades and compliments felt, they were short lived, easily cancelled out by a disapproving glance or hearing about unkind words whispered behind your back.

I had lost my north star. Before my illness, I was living every day in the past, imitating past versions of myself, and telling myself the same stories. I was wrapped in the comfort and security of ego and pain, hoping someone would see me.

'I forgot I could fly.'

I had always looked to God outside of myself. I looked to the heavens, and in buildings. I tried to find meaning and understanding in someone else's written word. I often referred to Creator Spirit, but not specifically God, when discussing beliefs with others. I was now able to recognize and *"say God"* with conviction and connection. God is a living creative force inside, flowing in and through me. I began to see the way, but it wasn't a new knowing, it was a remembrance ... I felt a spark of hope and light. I had never been alone.

It wasn't a giant moment, it was more like a quiet, gentle voice guiding me with love, and it gets stronger every day. Life is magical; gratitude is a superpower; I trust myself. I can't express the relief and ease that comes with acceptance, alignment, and living with intention, all sourced with love from God. All we have, is now, this moment, to create with God, and connect with each other.

A very difficult thing I came to know along the way, is that not everyone is meant to take this journey with you. You will lose people and you will walk away from things that you no longer feel connected to. Others will not understand your journey or why you changed, as they are on their own path and timeline. The loss is not a dramatic or a bad break up, it's a gradual fade away until you are left with a void. Empty spaces are a wonderful place to rest, pray, create and you will find new purpose and people to fill those spaces with love and joy.

I am dreaming again of things that I thought had long passed me by, like writing and serving others. I am willing to put myself out there for opportunities I have always been afraid to ask for. I am also so very blessed to have a wonderful circle of family and friends who unconditionally love and lift me.

My journey of healing is ongoing and never ends; working through pain is so very difficult. You will level up, each time gaining greater understanding.

The triggers don't go away, but I can recognize them now, so when I feel negative emotions, I lean into the discomfort to understand the source of my unease. The other great thing I learned is that I am lighter. I no longer feel the need to work on myself and heal daily which at times has been deep and dark. I live my life with joy and ease. I am present.

I don't think there was any other way to turn my life around; I am blessed to be alive and realize this gift I have been given. I found my way home. I remembered how to live.

Through God all things are possible.
[Matthew 19 :26].

I AM Poem by Jill Cornell (c)2022

I AM
Beautiful, a dreamer, a lover of light
I AM
Blessed, kind, helpful and wise
Two simple words that unite to transform
This world and all I can be
I will invite my soul's wonder to life
For what follows I AM will find me

I AM
Loyal and true, confident, talented, brave
I AM
A masterpiece, and in His image, I'm made
Words are electric when said with intent

Affirmed by no one but me
I choose whatever comes after I AM
Just as I say, it will be

I AM
Passionate, grateful, on fire inside
I AM
Here in the now, and full of surprise.
Two simple words that unite to transform
This world and all I can be
I will invite my soul's wonder to life
For what follows I AM will find me

I AM
A mother, daughter, wife, sister, friend
I AM
Forgiving, open, a love with no end
Words are electric when said with intent
Affirmed by no one but me
I choose whatever comes after I AM
Just as I say, it will be
What follows I AM will find me

I AM, I believe
I AM
Jill

Chapter Twelve

Divorce, Lilacs, Whispers, and my Friend Elijah

Tamara Hiller

"Everyone has a story as compelling and complicated as yours."

This is my story. A story that may be, on the surface, remarkably common but, for me, is intensely personal. As I reflect, God's nudges were intentional through the *gentle whispers* and divine moments—curated equitably by His grace. Eleven years later, I am happily situated on the other side of the storm. It feels like a blur. It feels like God.

"For I know the plans I have for you," declares the Lord, "plans to prosper you and not harm you, plans to give you hope and a future. (Jeremiah 29:11, NIV)

Humans are funny creatures. At times we are entirely self-absorbed. We are blinded by illusory beliefs that *our* power moves mountains at other times.

I believe God draws our attention in ways that are unique and personal. God helps us identify false ideas and beliefs that hinder our connection with Him.

I scripted a life of perfection in childhood, typical of the ideal middle-class white picket fence world view. I would attain a reputable career as a physician, marry well, and create a family. We would travel and live comfortably. Aside from a few twists and turns, I made a parallel reality.

Instead of obtaining a doctorate, I married a doctor. With this being said, I did not ignore my education, as I achieved a master's degree in Molecular Pathology by the age of twenty-five. We raised three beautiful children and traveled extensively. Early on in my marriage, desperate for the *white picket fence* narrative, I purchased the fence to delude myself and others about the reality of my life.

Currently, my life is a work in progress, progressing in a perfectly imperfect manner.

I married at the tender age of twenty-three. I was naïve and possessed minimal independent living skills. I met my now ex-husband during my university undergrad. When we started dating, he was 29 and a first-year medical student. There were red flags, gut prompts, and incidents that should have stopped me in my tracks and ended the relationship before we exchanged vows.

I felt I poorly measured up to his standards and was regularly blamed for my inadequacy. I was faulted for hypersensitivity and lacking a sense of humour. Actions and words often did not align, and the "goalpost" of expectations frequently changed.

One of the foundational issues in our marriage was that we did not share the same faith. I was raised by a family grounded in Christian beliefs, whereas his family viewed Christianity as a negative attribute. I blissfully ignored the relational warning signs and rationalized reasons to convince myself why it would work. I turned from my faith until the culmination of events brought me to my knees.

My aspirations to attend medical school were foiled and needed to find a different career path. Shortly after we were married, I was accepted into graduate school.

The constant attention required to "manage" my dating relationship caused irrevocable harm to my GPA. I recall coming home from school in tears, upset because research was not my passion. I knew that I needed to change faculties and pursue a degree in nursing. Financial restrictions forced me to remain in my current studies—and a well-paying studentship—that would bridge us until my husband could start his residency. Our budget did not allow me to switch programs, nor could it accommodate equal academic fulfillment. As a wife, I felt it was my responsibility to make personal sacrifices to support my marriage.

Not long after, I became pregnant with our first daughter. I remember feeling tight in my chest and hearing an intrinsic voice that said, *"It's not about you anymore."* The evening my water broke was poignant. A hurtful conversation with my husband grossly overshadowed the joy of becoming a mother during his on-call shift at the hospital. Our daughter was born through tears of joy and despair, and a new chapter of my life began. I silently prayed to God that night, begging for help and comfort. I heard nothing but silence and felt utterly deserted. That was the last prayer I uttered for approximately ten years.

Not long after our daughter was born, I became pregnant with our son. Currently, I was nearing the end of my graduate studies. My husband's residency was almost finished, and it was time for him to find employment. Growing up in a small town prompted my husband to gravitate to rural medicine opportunities. He wanted us to move to the country and promised we would move back to the city if things didn't pan out. The caveat was that after writing my graduate thesis, the chances of using my degree would be next to nil if we lived rural.

I will never forget the final meeting with my department chair when I shared the news of our decision to move. His response was, *"I wish you success in supporting your husband in his new career."* He then asked me to leave his office. Oomph! After exploring our options, we moved to a small town in Southwestern Ontario. Despite the adjustment, we found a wonderful place to live and established new roots of our own. Our son was born shortly after we moved. Two years later, our third child, another daughter, was born.

I met friends through a local support group for moms and tots during that time. These women were a gift from God and connected with them deeply. We offered mutual encouragement as we learned how to raise our children and become mothers in our own right. Not to mention so much laughter and tears. We still maintain contact, and I am deeply grateful for their support.

The cracks in my marriage grew in depth and breadth. It became increasingly evident that my husband and I viewed core issues differently: parenting, family goals, self-improvement, and finances. *Religious beliefs followed suit.* I was losing myself. It happened both slowly and all at once. The *white picket fence* narrative was a farce, but I was in too deep to retreat.

I never thought about homeschooling the children until it came time to sign them up for traditional school. It made sense. I would have a *purpose*, a job. We would gain more control over our *family time*—my husband spent a lot of time working at the hospital.

I met a woman at our daughters' dance class who befriended me and became a close friend during this time. She was open about her Christian beliefs, and our friendship seemed effortless. Our families started spending time together and creating fun-filled memories. I believe God used her to draw me near to Him. One day she asked if I would come to her women's Bible study. I said, "Yes," before allowing any time to think or decline. It was the perfect combination of *my life unraveling* and an invitation to *rest in Him*.

Walking through the church doors felt weird and awkward, yet eerily familiar.

Once again, I was surrounded by a church family, which felt amazing. Our children began attending both church and youth events. They developed a personal relationship with God. God did not forget me, and I was reminded once again that God will relentlessly pursue a relationship with *his* children.

The hardest part about going back to church was being prompted to pray. It just felt odd plus I was ashamed. I walked away and remained silent with God for over a decade. My friend said, *"It's okay. God knows what you are feeling. He already knows your life's events and feelings!"* I had nothing to lose, so I started to pray. For a short time, God answered my prayers and I felt close to Him.

I've learned that prayers come in a variety of forms. There are your *"garden variety"* prayers which includes safety for your loved ones or petitioning for miracles and cures. There are prayers uttered while stirring soup on the stove—chattering about everything and nothing. We may exercise prayer while driving to work, asking God to help us *hold space* for others. Some prayers are born from the silence because no words can articulate the current situation. Then there are the prayers of the broken hearted that are formed in tears. Tears are prayers too.

As my relationship with God strengthened, my marriage blew up behind closed doors. Call it what you want, spiritual warfare or reaping the consequences of being *unequally yoked*; I heard it all.

My emotional, mental and physical health spiraled downwards rapidly. I became depressed and experienced frequent panic attacks. My weight plummeted, my gut health deteriorated, and food sensitivities emerged. I weighed less than one hundred pounds. I cried daily and my prayers bounced off the ceiling. God was silent—very silent. Psalm 34:18 says *"The Lord is close to the brokenhearted and saves those who are crushed in spirit"*

Trials often present a *pivotal moment* that induces the motivation to change. At the time, I was done! I felt like a failure. My marriage was over, and I was confident the kids would be better off without me. I was convinced God had abandoned me and was attending to more important issues.

'Indeed, He could better use His time than deal with my hopeless situation.'

There was only one solution. My life was worthless and ending it would solve my problems. I had a plan. The decision was made. I began to weep behind my closed bedroom door. My six-year-old daughter slipped a note under the door at that exact moment.

God reworked my story through our daughter and changed my mind. I found peace in that moment of divine intervention. Unbeknownst to me, it was the calm before the storm. Things were about to take a turn for the worse.

As I began experiencing increased depression, anxiety and panic attacks, I scheduled an appointment with my family doctor to discuss my situation. I felt ashamed and embarrassed. No one knew my secret. '*Would he think I was crazy*?'

The doctor sat down, listened, and offered support. I gleaned pharmacological support through antidepressant and anti-anxiety medications. I ended up taking these medications for the next four years which helped me weather the worst of the storm.

At that time, I decided to end my marriage. I felt afraid to move forward. *'How would I tell my husband, children, community, or the members of my evangelical church?'*

Of all the individuals in the Bible, Elijah is my person. I do not know if I chose him, or he chose me. One June morning, while driving into town to pick up eyeglasses at the optometrist, I pictured being six years old again—life was simple. I imagined being transported back to Winnipeg. I remembered walking to school, smelling the lilacs, and hoping I wouldn't be late for school.

As I continued my drive into town, I prayed without ceasing. I was perturbed, once again feeling like my prayers were bouncing off the ceiling. Increased frustration triggered a temper tantrum, and I started yelling at God. My thoughts flashed to a prior conversation with a friend regarding my hesitation to engage in prayer—equally applicable in this situation.

'I had nothing to lose, and He knew how I felt, right?'

I held nothing back. I insisted on an answer from God and equally noted that I would greatly appreciate a sign! I am confident it was quite a sight to behold.

Arriving at my destination, I parked the car and concluded my rant. I ascended the stairs to the optometrist's office with my head held low. Suddenly, I was assaulted with the smell of lilacs! Raising my eyes, I observed a massive bouquet of lilacs on the counter.

Chills ran down my spine, and I experienced intense shivers and goosebumps. I paid for my new prescription sunglasses and raced home.

Arriving home, I felt compelled to open my Bible but didn't know what to reference because I wasn't well versed in the Word—a newbie. So, I randomly opened my Bible and it fell on the following passage from 1 Kings 19:3 *3 "Elijah was afraid and ran for his life. When he came to Beersheba in Judah, he left his servant there, 4 while he himself went a day's journey into the wilderness. He came to a broom bush, sat down under it and prayed that he might die. "I have had enough, Lord," ... 9 And the word of the Lord came to him: "What are you doing here, Elijah?" 10 He replied, "I have been very zealous for the Lord God Almighty. The Israelites have rejected your covenant, torn down your altars, and put your prophets to death with the sword. I am the only one left, and now they are trying to kill me too. 11 The Lord said, "Go out and stand on the mountain in the presence of the Lord, for the Lord is about to pass by." Then a great and powerful wind tore the mountains apart and shattered the rocks before the Lord, but the Lord was not in the wind. After the wind there was an earthquake, but the Lord was not in the earthquake. 12 After the earthquake came a fire, but the Lord was not in the fire. And after the fire came a gentle whisper."*

So, one point for God and zero for Tamara. I desperately needed that lesson, delivered by appearing to me in lilacs was life-changing—and personally tailored to me and me alone.

'I wanted to die. I was zealous for God. I was in the depths of despair. I demanded a sign. '

God had not abandoned me, nor was He disappointed in the messiness of my life. Thinking that God needed to shake me harshly was a distorted truth. I needed a Fatherly touch, a gentle hug, and a soft voice. I needed confirmation that He was *with me in the fire.*

I mustered up the courage to speak my truth—to my husband, children, friends, and church family. It did not go well.

That summer, I traveled to Winnipeg on three different occasions. I felt led to go back home. I was in survival mode. It was primal. I was running solely on body memory recalling the last place I was happy. Perhaps a new framework would support me in rebuilding a life for my children and me. Relocating to the city I first knew as home would allow me to pursue an education in nursing—it was my only hope. A career in nursing would provide an opportunity to become self-sufficient and financially stable. For whatever reason, my husband agreed to move back to Winnipeg. I was shocked. In my opinion, this was the only concession he made in terms of our divorce.

My prayer life began to change, consisting of two auto-repeat prayers. *'If I am doing the wrong thing, stop me hard. If I am doing Your will, please provide.'*

I was in awe that the move to Winnipeg presented a literal *parting of the sea* effect. On my final visit back home to Winnipeg before our final move, I was praying to God about the house we just put up for sale in Ontario. Two minutes after I settled into my seat for the flight, my phone rang, it was my ex-husband. Our house in Ontario had a buyer offering the list price. Two days later, God provided approval with the provision of the ideal home I envisioned purchasing; located in a specific area of town, close to green space, with four bedrooms, and close to a particular elementary school.

Before moving back to Winnipeg, I had to say goodbye to the life I had built in Ontario. In those final days, I discovered my true friends. People showed their true colours and were not shy about their thoughts and feelings! My true friends cried with me and hugged me tightly. I have returned several times to visit my supports in that small town, supports that are only a phone call away.

Most of my Christian friends did not support my decision to return to Winnipeg. I was shocked with the judgement and the less than Jesus' response that I received. They did not know my situation nor my story. The last church service I attended was both emotional and bittersweet. I was so thankful for this building and the people I met who welcomed me back into the faith. It was difficult and painful to see them literally turn their backs to me refusing to speak with me in deep disapproval but hugging the children saying their goodbyes. I prayed to God during that last service that I promised to be faithful as He has been faithful to me throughout my life. One of my favourite Hymns from childhood is "Great is thy Faithfulness". God "whispered" to me once again that day. Tears rolled down my face singing the closing hymn the worship team chose that Sunday:

Great is Thy faithfulness
Great is Thy faithfulness
Morning by morning, new mercies I see
All I have needed Thy hand hath provided
Great is Thy faithfulness, Lord, unto me!
Pardon for sin and a peace that endureth
Thine own dear presence to cheer and to guide
Strength for today and bright hope for tomorrow
Blessings all mine, with ten thousand beside!

Starting over was difficult. I knew it wouldn't be easy but never anticipated it being that hard. Trial after trial presented without relent. It felt like being hit with consecutive Tsunamis, devoid of time to catch my breath. Financially, I was hit with unexpected tax bills and mounting legal bills which accompanied the divorce proceedings. I was devastated by the lack of recognition for past academic accomplishments; apparently, there was a *'10-year rule'* in the Faculty of Nursing. An inactive academic status greater than ten years warranted that I would have to retake previously completed courses. After a good cry (or two), I dried my tears and got to work. I realized that repeating the intro biology classes helped renew my confidence in hindsight. Every 'A' earned grew my faith and ability to recreate my life. Extrinsic circumstances pressed in, but my cognitive ability to endure and focus would, one day, promote self-sufficiency.

God is faithful. His provision sustained my ability to cover expenses, food, and clothing for my family. There was never a dime to spare, but He provided what I needed. I asked for a provision. He granted my request.

"Ask, and you shall receive." (Matthew 7:7)

The lowest point of my journey was navigating relationships with the children. The collateral damage from the divorce was devastating. My rapport with their father was likely to remain one of *high conflict / low contact*. I was mindful not to disparage the children's father. If I couldn't speak positively or neutral, I said nothing.

Unfortunately, the mindfulness was not reciprocated. This, in turn, provided the children with an incomplete version of the story. A story that, to date, will never be fully understood. There are parts of the story I will take to my grave. Sharing certain events would not change the past. Nor would it change the course of events that unfolded.

Divorce is troublesome for children, regardless of age. Parents are encouraged to always think of the best interest of the child.

Although they are now grown and have flown the nest, they are still and will always be children of divorce and you do not place adult issues on children. Period.

One of the children took the divorce particularly hard. I recall an unforgettable conversation while sitting in my parked car in a parking lot of a strip mall.

My child said, *"Mom, I am so angry about this divorce. I want someone to blame. So, I am choosing you. I need to choose you."*

I spent precisely eight hours with that child during the next five years, most of which occurred on Christmas Day. My ex-husband did little to encourage reconciliation. Despite attempts to block them out of my thoughts, my heart hurt daily. The key to coping was learning to hold space for the hurt until time presented an opportunity for reconnection. Grace was both an unexpected lesson and a gift.

I was accepted into nursing school and graduated. One of my friends from Ontario flew in and saw me accept my new shiny degree. Other unanticipated blessings were sprinkled along the way while I retrained, particularly in terms of travel. Travel has always been a primary method of self-care I have used throughout my life. I often need to go far away so that I can come back and slay more dragons. Travel allows me to be free of roles that I have as a mother, daughter, friend or nurse. It also allows me to learn about different cultures so that I can incorporate the teachings into my everyday life. In my solo travels, I have learned confidence in how to trouble shoot in all sorts of situations. I was so grateful that during my time in nursing school, I was given the opportunity to use my travel points and win a studentship to travel to Europe, Cambodia, China and Bali for minimal expense.

In the last year, I am happy to share that my estranged relationship with that child has begun to mend. It has been a very slow process. The divorce is now final, which took over nine years to complete. It is not easy when the legal system supports an environment of whereby one party can unleash their discontent on the other without ceasing. The lawyers were the only ones that won with the endless dollars that were billed throughout the entire process. The bills have slowly but surely been paid off and I am now transitioning from survival mode to that of absolute thriving.

Psalm 23:4-5 [4] "*Even though I walk through the valley of the shadow of death, I will fear no evil, for you are with me; your rod and your staff, they comfort me.*

[5] *You prepare a table before me in the presence of my enemies.*"

God has begun to restore the estranged relationship with my child. It has been a slow but steady process. After a nine-year trek, the divorce is finally complete. The onslaught of legal bills has slowly been paid off. I am transitioning from survival mode to that of absolute thriving.

Now employed as a palliative care nurse, I have been helping patients and their families with *end-of-life care* for the past six years. I have learned that God is the Master Physician specializing in person-centered care. Palliative care is embedded within four tenants—physical, emotional, mental, and spiritual well-being. It is dedicated to finding ways to ease suffering and increase the quality of life. I am convinced that God led me to this field to palliate others while, in turn, He continues to palliate me.

I have learned to love and trust again within the context of a romantic relationship. God has given me a second chance. At first, I was skeptical, always waiting for the other shoe to drop. My current partner does not have a *hidden agenda* and continually *shares space* with me. He continues to demonstrate care and concern for the children and me. He has built a healthy relationship with the children. He has made clear that his role is not to be their dad but to be another cheerleader, support person and sounding board in their lives.

God understands His children. This includes His expectations with respect for having a perfect faith that one day it will all work itself out. Many a day I only have the faith capacity the size of a mustard seed (Matthew 17:20). Other days, my faith is bolder. God was, is and will always be okay with that truth. Hebrews 11:1 says, *"Faith is the confidence in what we hope for and assurance about what we do not see."* I do not know God's plans for me, but His transforming power inspires me. I have learned to continue, in faith, believing His plans are for me, prosper me, and not harm me.

So, stay tuned, friends. He plans to give *us* hope and a future.

God Bless, Tamara Hiller RN, MSc. (Pathology)

Chapter Thirteen

Some Rainbows Have Polka Dots

Gloria Schellhorn Lecomte

My name is Gloria Audrey Schellhorn Lecomte. I am 86 years young, born in 1936. Several memories came to mind when asked to write a chapter for Chasing Rainbows. I decided to write about a childhood experience, as it set the tone for most of the storms to come.

I was the eldest of five children: one sister and three brothers—Iona, Richard, Wayne, and Jack. We grew up on a grain farm in Carrot River, Saskatchewan.

I spent most of my childhood working on the farm and going to school. My neighbours, who lived half a mile away, and the farm animals, were my only friends. I was especially fond of a Pomeranian poodle named Teddy.

Unbeknownst to Teddy, he was not the typical choice for a farm dog. Teddy would sit bravely on the front porch, ready to defend the house at all costs. He would present a ferocious snarl while barking at coyotes and bears from the safety of the front porch. When he sensed his predators getting close, he would suddenly utter a high pitch squeal in a desperate plea to come in the house.

On one occasion, my mother beckoned us to observe Teddy sleeping on the front porch. He was oblivious to the presence of a giant bear about to step over him. Teddy, the protector, slept right through it!

Teddy and I had a few things in common. Teddy was a fierce protector, and I was a hardworking farm labourer. Neither of us fit the typical profile of our positions, but alas, we did well to prove we were capable candidates. My physique was built and strong. I could work the farm as well as any man, and I took pride in that.

One day, my mother called my Aunt Annie to ask if I could move in with her.

Mom stated,

"Gloria's father, Fred, treats Gloria like a man and is overworking her."

I enjoyed being capable of doing a man's work, especially when women were expected in the kitchen. In hindsight, my physical capabilities were a rainbow in the making; I learned that an optimistic attitude presents limitless opportunities.

Later in life, the local news wrote a story recognizing that I was the first woman to pump gas in Saskatoon! The farm work that my father entrusted me with allowed me to develop deep-rooted confidence.

I learned about God from my mother and attendance at a summer *church school*. My daily trek to school was an hour in duration. I enjoyed school and looked forward to graduating. However, my father had other ideas.

When I was fifteen, my father announced that it was time to grow up; a woman's role was to get married and have babies. He wasn't a mean-spirited man. He grew up in a time when these were expectations of "*good*" women. I pleaded with him to allow me to finish school.

That night he dropped me off at the train station with a twenty-dollar bill and said, *"Honey, when you get a job, I want this back."*

I adamantly ensured he got that twenty dollars back.

My heart was crushed. Fear overwhelmed every inch of my being. This storm gob smacked me!

The train ride to the city was lonely, but the conductor was a kind man who ensured my safety and gave me juice to drink. Arriving at my predetermined destination, I found myself in the city of Saskatoon at 10:30 p.m. and homeless.

Alone and afraid, I silently prayed for help. I needed a safe place to stay. I walked the streets until I came to 25th Street East. To my left were several row houses.

Walking down the road, I noticed that one of the homes was well-lit and appeared inviting. I knocked on the door and asked if I could spend the night. A tall, heavy-built man answered the door and glared at me momentarily.

He said, *"Yeah kid, what do you want?"*

Frightened, I quietly replied, *"I don't have anywhere to sleep tonight."*

Puzzled, he said, *"Just one second.* Suddenly, he yelled, *Stella!"*

A short, kind-looking woman came to the door and said, *"Yes, Jimmy?"*

He said, *"This kid says she has nowhere to sleep. What do we do?"*

She looked at me, and in a beautiful Norwegian accent, said, *"Yes, my dear. You can come in. I'll make you coffee and something to eat. You can sleep in young Jimmy's bed; he will be away for two nights."*

That became my home for the next two years. My experience living with this couple paved the way for enduring the future storms in my life.

Years later, I married and had four boys: Mitchell, Perry, Lamont, and Dean. The boys have since grown up to become extraordinary gentlemen. Three of the boys are married with children and grandchildren of their own. Dean and his wife have fur babies.

I have experienced illness and loss. I have observed storms come to pass. I learned there is glory in the struggle and power in overcoming. In hindsight, I became aware of God's ever-present faithfulness along my journey.

God blessed me abundantly. I believe God allowed my experience of feeling discarded at the train station to prepare me for what was to come.

I did get married, have a beautiful family, and spent 25 years as a restauranteur. My father, though well-intentioned, was incorrect. I was created for more than the words he spoke over me.

Later in life, my father became a police officer and a highly esteemed community member. He studied and successfully graduated from the Police Academy with a grade three education. He looked out for youth, often diverting them from unhealthy life choices. He demonstrated that God makes a way out of no way.

At the age of fifty, I felt led, by the Lord, to go back to school. With a grade eight education and mature student designation, I was accepted into university. I obtained a graduate degree and became an ordained minister.

I received employment as a Chaplin at a local prison. The same frightened little girl who felt alone in the world grew up to become a prison minister.

Utilizing my experience, strength, and hope, I encouraged men who felt isolated and fearful. I shared about connection with an unfailing, personal relationship with God. A Father who would never discard them; instead, he would permeate them with a love that would heal a broken spirit. *"And we know that in all things God works for the good of those who love him, who have been called according to his purpose." Romans 8:28*

God uses every situation, good or bad, to lead us to our purpose. We can never be wholly lost to Him.

I am now an 86-year-old retired minister living in a retirement community in Ontario. I am currently in the process of moving back home to be closer to family. It is difficult leaving life and friends in Ontario.

Am I afraid? Sure. But I know that God has a plan and a purpose.

I will have the opportunity to be with my family during my golden years. I look forward to spending time with my family, children, grandchildren, and great-grandchildren.

Life involves change; it contains storms and is full of rainbows. We can choose to focus on the darkened storms or vibrant rainbows. I decide to chase vibrant rainbows—covered in polka dots! Spoken from 86 years of experience, your life will be fulfilled if you choose to chase rainbows.

Love Gloria

Chapter Fourteen

Finding Power in the Storm

Wendy Noll

'LINGUISTIC RELATIVITY IS FASCINATING, to say the least. The word storm in Hebrew, הרעס, *means to take by force. In the literal sense, a storm is an atmospheric development of precipitation often accompanied by wind. Figuratively, the word storm has a negative, hectic connotation and is associated with sadness, chaos, hardship, or foreboding omens.'*

Scripture presents no single word that is translated as 'miracle.' There are four primary Greek words translated as a miracle: works (ergon), wonders (teras), powers (dunamis), and signs (semelon). The English word, 'miracle,' comes from the Latin term miraculum—something that evokes wonder.

These various representations are used because no single term can exhaust all the significance of a miracle.'

Do you ever consider the reality of how fast life can change? Have you experienced miracles amidst the storms of life?

On the morning of March 4, 2020, an unprecedented storm ravished the core of my being.

The rising of the sun brought forth the blessing of a new day, an opportunity to lift the will and glory of God. Upon awakening, I snuggled with my puppy, pondered gratitude reflections, and sent my husband a sappy message.

Ping! Ping! Ping! Excitedly, I reached for my phone anticipating our morning ritual of playful bantering.

Glaring at the screen, I read, "*In a hospital.*"

My thoughts sped into overdrive like a hamster wheeling on steroids. I began ruminating on an internal dialogue.

'What does that mean? Oh God, what's happening? Is he in a hospital serving legal documents? Is he in a hospital? He doesn't see a doctor unless the presenting symptoms are urgent!'

Shaking violently, I tried to respond to his message. Tears were running down my cheeks, hindering my ability to read what I was typing.

Desperate, I cried, "*God, PLEASE help me.*"

I cried to my dog, "*Oh Bella, what is going on?*"

I couldn't stop shaking long enough to navigate a legible message!

Unable to send a message, I called Dale. After several rings, Dale answered, "*...uh...huh...ah...hello.*"

"*Hi, Dale? What's going on?*"

"*Hi...I can't talk...uh, I can't breathe...pain.*"

"*What do you mean? I don't understand. Dale, where are you?*"

"*I am at the hospital...I am having trouble talking. I will message you.*"

"Dale, wait. I don't know where you are. What hospital?"

The phone line went dead. I stared at the screen, shaking uncontrollably. I managed to send a message asking Dale for the hospital's name.

Ping! Finally, I received the name of a Toronto hospital.

I replied, "*I am on my way, babe. I love you.*"

Ping! Dale replied, "*I love you too.*"

In a heightened emotional state, I began to panic. I didn't know who to call. I was in no condition to drive. My daughter was working in Toronto. I called my son.

Steven answered, "*Hey ma, what's up?*"

Pausing to gather my thoughts, I said, "*Steven? Steven, I need to get to the hospital. Dale is in the hospital. I don't know what's happening, but I need a ride. I can't drive.*"

Recalling that my son had not renewed his driver's license, I called my girlfriend. Jane answered, "*Hello, girlfriend. How are you?*"

I replied, "*Jane! Jane, Dale's in the hospital. I need a ride; I'm in no shape to drive.*"

Jane said, "*I will be right over!*"

My memory of the drive to the hospital is a blur; I vaguely recall speaking with Dale's son. Moments blended, and hours stood still. We arrived at the hospital in record time. Jane dropped me off at the emergency department door and left to park the car.

Racing to the information desk, I was immediately directed to Dale's room. As I observed the medical team attend to his surmounting needs, I felt a rush of emotions lodged in my throat. Holding back tears, I walked toward him and met his embrace.

I quickly shifted my attention to my daughter, who had arrived half an hour prior. She seemed to be managing her experience of the situation by mindlessly scrolling through social media feeds.

Dale's tolerance to pain is extremely high. He practices prayer and mind control as preferred pain management tools and avoids pharmacological remedies at all costs.

I felt helplessness trying to overtake me as I watched him desperately fighting to manage excruciating pain levels.

Jane entered the room relaxed and proceeded to redirect Dale's attention to trivial, humorous engagement. Jane has a background in nursing and is well versed in emergency protocols. As I observed her body language, I did not detect any indication of palpable fear. Her demeanour had a calming effect on my ever-rising anxiety levels.

The medical team frequented his room to perform vitals and monitor his pain levels. One of the nurses informed Dale that the doctor approved medication as an option for pain management. As a recovered opiate addict, Dale struggled with consenting to the use of narcotics to assist in reducing his pain levels.

Turning to me, he asked, "*If I take morphine, is that considered a relapse?*"

I said, "*Dale, you are notably experiencing incredible pain levels. You're in a hospital, advised by a medical team to utilize prescribed medication. It will be administered and monitored by professionals. From my perspective, that is not considered a relapse.*"

Dale's inability to manage the pain became increasingly unbearable, and he succumbed to the use of medication. After several doses of narcotics, Dale reported the medicine offered minimal effectiveness.

'*Being re-exposed to opioids or untreated pain is a common fear in those choosing to abstain from their drug of choice. Compounded fear of discrimination and withdrawal adds to the intrinsic complexities. Not to mention the systemic effects of toxins on the intricate mechanics of the human body.*'

'Do you ever wonder what the body's primary function is? Essentially the human body is intricately designed to heal itself. Each day humans are awakened by God, and their bodies commence to respond to the environment and maintain homeostasis. A body depleted of naturally produced pain killers seeks external pain relief.

The essence of humanity is complicated—seven billion human forms occupying a complex universe while transforming billions of energy-carrying molecules.

Ad infinitum, seven billion minds produce an average of 60,000 thoughts per day with a projected response of feelings and behaviours.

Amplified by the complexities of variant stressors and the increasing level of atrocities in the world, people succumb to a litany of coping mechanisms in a vain attempt to reduce pain. As the levels of pain increase worldwide, the systemic response is that of an increased dose of one's numbing agent to produce immediate gratification.

Stressors are the body's response to threats or danger—whether perceived or real. Addiction moves one away from pain and toward pleasure. Addiction works until it doesn't!'

Perhaps the answer to the addiction conundrum is restoration of healthy family systems.

My son arrived at the hospital within the hour. He coordinated a ride with a friend and, upon entering the room, appeared to be abruptly slapped into a state of shock. He seemed to choke back a tear and managed his emotions with deflections of humour.

The medical team advised limiting visitors because my husband's condition was critical. Adhering to hospital protocol, I embraced our family members with an exchange of hugs and encouragement. I returned to the room and sat by Dale's bedside.

Suddenly, the room filled with medical team members, and we were advised that Dale was being admitted to the intensive care unit (ICU).

Dale, engrossed in his pain, seemed oblivious to the situation's intensity. He maintained a state of optimism and humour despite unimaginable suffering. I was in awe of his unwavering faith.

Arriving at the ICU, I was directed to the waiting room while they attended to Dale's critical care needs. I was informed that I would receive a call when I could join him in ICU.

I was vaguely aware of my surroundings as I collapsed into one of the waiting room chairs. I felt physically exhausted and emotionally drained. Zoning into my environment, I heard the faint sound of music. It was a familiar song, Break Every Chain, by Jesus Culture. Lifting my eyes, I saw a lady across from me and a man seated at the opposite end of the room.

I said, "*Excuse me, can you increase the volume, please?*"

The lady began to turn the volume down. I immediately responded, "*No, can you turn the volume up, please.*"

Suddenly the man across the room said, "*Ma, she asked you to turn the sound UP.*"

Settling into my chair, I felt overcome by the presence of God. The lyrics, "*There is power in the name of Jesus,*" saturated my mind as I prayerfully meditated on His name. The peace of God that transcends understanding permeated my being, and I felt a sense of ease and comfort. Oddly, I had no desire to contact others; I simply longed to marinate in His presence.

Ring! Ring! Ring! I was startled by the ring tone of a nearby phone. I answered, "*Hello.*"

A lady responded, "*Is this Wendy?*"

I said, "*Yes.*"

She instructed, "*Please follow sanitary protocols, enter the ICU, and head directly to your husband's room.*"

As I hung up the phone, I paused to acknowledge feelings of fear and anxiety about the uncertainty of what might come.

Walking into the Dale's room, I experienced the paradox of internal catatonia amidst robotic movement toward his bedside chair. I battled waves of emotional turmoil.

The room was inundated with machines, wires, tubes, and medical supplies. It housed an eerie silence despite the rhythmic sound of medical chimes. The overwhelming smell of antiseptic was both pleasant and disturbing. I longed to taste the sweetness of his kiss and weave our bodies in an eternal embrace. Feeling beckoned by the gentle tap of his finger, I awakened from a trance-like state. I squeezed his hand in response to his touch.

In a whisper, he said, "*Hi, babe. How long have I been asleep?*"

I said, "*You have slept sporadically for several hours.*"

He said, "*It must be late; it's dark outside.*"

I said, "*Get some rest, babe. I will be here when you wake up.*"

Noticing my exhaustion, the ICU staff encouraged me to return home (over two hours away). After expressing my intent to remain by my husband's side, they wheeled a hospital cot into the room so I could sleep. As I stretched my aching body, I felt a depth of gratitude.

Solely focused on my husband's breathing, I nodded in and out of consciousness. My dream state was erratic and pervaded by nightmares. Tossing and turning, I explored numerous relaxation techniques in an attempt to fall asleep. Finally, I surrendered my efforts to God.

I exploded into prayer, wrestling with Him to comprehend the magnitude of the situation.

I cried out, "*God, I am angry! I am overcome by fear and despair. Where are you in this situation? How could you allow this to happen? I prayed for a God-fearing man for six years. Finally, you bless me with the love of my life, and five years later…?*"

Sobbing uncontrollably, I couldn't finish the sentence. I didn't want the utterance of my cries to awaken Dale. I refused to express my deepest fear verbally. Life and death are in the power of the tongue [Proverbs 18:21], and I am determined to speak life over my husband.

I began warring in prayer, "*God, you can have my house and all my earthly belongings. Please, I beg you, DON'T TAKE MY HUSBAND! Please, Oh God, have mercy. God, I can't stay in this world without him. Please, Papa, don't leave me here alone.*"

Words cannot express the depth of my emotional pain. I was undone. In desperation, I reached out to numerous prayer warriors, asking them to join me in prayer. My phone began to blow up with confirmation that hundreds of believers were storming heaven's gates, claiming God's promises over Dale.

Wearied from sleep deprivation, I drifted into a state of unconsciousness. Faint hues of daylight began to seep through the blinds as the earth dawned a new day.

'*In the blink of an eye, the winds of change can redirect our path in life. Crisis creates the illusory experience of the stillness of time. In these moments, we often pause to reflect on the fragility of life; we are finite beings. Often, during these times, we experience a shift in perspective.*'

Awakened by the muffled sound of voices, I paused to focus and wipe crusted tears from the corner of my eye.

Dale said, "*Good morning, my love. Did you sleep well?*"

I said, "*Good morning, babe. How are you feeling?*"

Turning to Dale's primary nurse, I asked, "*What is the prognosis of my husband's condition? Are there any updates? Have the doctors determined what is causing the severity of his pain?*"

The nurse said, "*The doctor will be in to see Dale later this morning.*"

Dale thanked the nurse and said, "*I didn't sleep well; the pain is still pretty severe.*"

Dale drifted off to sleep, and I remained by his side. Breaking the silence, the doctor entered the room and announced his arrival. "*Hello Dale. How are you feeling?*" he asked.

Sarcastically, Dale replied, "*Never felt better, doctor.*"

The doctor explained Dale's diagnosis and the critical nature of his condition. Dale was diagnosed with pericarditis—inflammation of the thin, protective, bag-like membrane surrounding the heart. There was a tear in the membrane surrounding Dale's heart. He needed to be transported to another hospital via ambulance to receive an angiogram. The angiogram would determine whether Dale required heart surgery.

Both hospitals ramped up their screening protocols because Canada was facing the onset of the Covid pandemic.

Dale was prepped and wheeled into the surgical unit, where he awaited the angiogram. I was directed to a surgical waiting room where I anxiously awaited the outcome—alone.

Within an hour, I was called to the post-surgical unit. As I approached Dale's room, I noticed he appeared different; his face was glowing!

I said, "*Hi, babe, how was the procedure?*"

Dale said, "*I feel good; the pain has decreased substantially.*"

I said, "*That's great news. Did you receive surgery?*"

He replied, "*They didn't do anything. God miraculously healed me! The doctors performed the angiogram and discovered the leak was healed; the camera detected recent scar tissue, thus providing confirmation.*"

"*What! I don't understand. Are they sure? How is that possible?*"

"*God healed me, babe. I can go home.*"

Just then, the doctor entered the room.

He said, "*We do not have a rational, medical explanation for Dale's healing. Your husband had a tear and was bleeding in places he shouldn't be but scarring somehow healed the injured site.*"

I said, "*So, he can go home?*"

The doctor replied, "*We want to keep him for observation for a couple of days, and then he is free to go home.*"

I said, "*Thank you, doctor.*"

Dale and I sat quietly as we processed the experience.

Two days later, we packed up our belongings, met with the doctor for prescribed aftercare, and headed home.

The drive home was surreal. Dale drove. The erratic fluctuations in emotional complexities overcame me, tears, shock, fear, and gratitude. In the months following Dale's miraculous healing, I experienced profound shifts in my worldview and contemplated life's fragility. I felt the essence of rainbow symbolism bridging fear and hope.

Throughout the Bible, there are numerous references to rainbow symbolism. Rainbows, though symbolic, are a magnificent phenomenon to observe.

The first mention of rainbows in the Bible occurs in Genesis 9:13; The Great Flood. God displayed His rainbow as a tangible sign of His covenant to us, His promise to never destroy the earth again with a worldwide flood.

The second mention takes place in Ezekiel's vision [Ezekiel 1:28]. Ezekiel was privileged to see a vision of God in heaven, and the brightness of God was seen as a rainbow.

The third reference to a rainbow was described as part of the manifestation of God [Revelation 4:3, 10:1].

Rainbows are symbolic of the masterful Creator [God] of nature; they represent bridges from earth to heaven and hold firm God's covenant promise to us.

As a witness to Dale's miraculous healing, I held firm to the power of God. The onset of a global pandemic crept around the world. All while fear and uncertainty mainstreamed media sources at an international level.

Initially, I fell privy to the status quo. In time, God began to permeate the atmosphere with His presence. He replayed the events of March fourth like a motion picture scrolling through my mind. Events that affirmed and strengthened my faith. Like creation, faith grows in darkness.

I pray that *you* the reader, embrace God's interwoven beauty reflected in the narratives of fourteen ordinary women.

Courageous women who trudged the storms of life and found their unique '*God smack*' at the end of the rainbow.

In Him, Wendy Noll

Manufactured by Amazon.ca
Bolton, ON

28899226R00092